*The
ill-spoken
Word*

The ill-spoken Word

THE DECLINE OF SPEECH IN AMERICA

Leonard A. Stevens

INTRODUCTION BY *Ralph G. Nichols*

McGraw-Hill Book Company

NEW YORK   LONDON   TORONTO

This book was dedicated to my wife, CARLA, *until she learned its title*

ACKNOWLEDGMENTS

The sources for this book are so many and so varied, spread over so many years, that it would be impossible to point to them all. Besides drawing on printed sources, a great deal of which are found in the bibliography, many of the ideas and factual material were developed through the very medium this book discusses, the spoken word. In my travels for several years as a reporter and writer, I met and talked with countless people in all walks of life in most every state of the United States. I frequently took the opportunity to discuss speech and what it meant to people. Three examples:

• One extensive assignment took me all over the nation with the engineers of a major petroleum company. I often talked about speech needs with them and I know some of the conversations are reflected in these pages.

• One afternoon, while researching a recent book on human aging, I visited a Chicago psychiatrist, Jack Weinberg, who is famous in gerontology. Eventually we came to talk of speech and the interview spilled over into a patient's appointment time. I hope both Dr. Weinberg and his patient forgive me, for the extended talk was useful and I know it is reflected between these book covers.

• At a luncheon one noon at the National Bureau of Standards in Washington, I asked six well-known scientists to discuss my topic. It turned out that they were deeply concerned about this form of communication and they had much to offer my efforts.

Without further belaboring such informal research, let

me say in summary that nearly everyone I met for five or six years was a potential source for this volume. I feel it was an important part of my effort because speech, as the book emphasizes, is everyone's business nearly all of the time.

If I had to trace my interest and concern for the spoken word to one man, it would not be difficult—though the individual named may be surprised to know about it. He is Orville Hitchcock of the University of Iowa. In only a few college speech courses taught by him I came by a sense of the importance of good speech that eventually had a lot to do with writing this book.

The person who wrote the accompanying introduction, another Iowa friend, Ralph G. Nichols, has also been a major contributor to my interest in the field of speech. Five years after leaving Iowa, we met at the University of Minnesota to co-author an article for *Collier's* magazine. Since then we have written a number of things together, including the book *Are You Listening?*

Besides writing the introduction here, Ralph contributed greatly as an editor, applying his extensive speech background to what I wrote. He worked on the book chapter by chapter as I wrote it—at his University of Minnesota desk, on his lap in airplanes and in hotel rooms. What he had to say led to considerable reorganization and rewriting. I know it is a different and better book because of his efforts. I extend my thanks to him once more.

The staffs of three libraries deserve a great deal of thanks for helping me with the research reflected by the bibliography: Danbury State College, Yale University and Columbia Teachers College.

I would like to thank William Work of the Speech Association of America for offering material and numerous suggestions to help with the research of the book.

Ellen Moore of New Milford contributed considerably to the book by patiently and diligently putting my heavily scribbled work copy into neatly typewritten form and then doing it all over again in revision.

My wife and four children certainly deserve mention for putting up with many hours of extra absenteeism during the writing of the book, and for living with my neglect of household maintenance duties on the same account.

Finally, may I throw a bouquet to a friend, Daniel Hotaling of Antioch College, who, on a recent vacation, found himself terribly trapped in having to listen to me read sections of this book, which at the moment was nearly completed.

Leonard A. Stevens

New Milford, Connecticut

Contents

INTRODUCTION

The sum total of human knowledge since the time of Christ may be represented as a tiny snowball resting at the top of a long, gentle mountain slope covered with snow. In the year One the snowball started to roll down the gentle slope. In 1,750 years it was double in weight and complexity because man now knew twice as much as he had known in the days of Christ.

But then the snowball suddenly began to pick up speed, spurred perhaps by the Industrial Revolution, when man's store of knowledge began to increase at a dramatic pace. By 1900 the snowball once more redoubled in weight and complexity, had a factor of four attached to it. Within fifty additional years, man's total knowledge had redoubled again; by 1950 it had a factor of eight attached to it. And in just ten more years, 1960, it had redoubled a third time and the growth factor had become one of sixteen.

COMMUNICATION IS BREAKING DOWN

Today we face an awesome problem: We have at least sixteen times as much to be taught and learned as at the time of Christ, but we certainly have *not* multiplied our communication and learning skills by any similar factor. Can any of us honestly argue that we now read, write with sixteen times the efficiency of Aristotle, Plato, or Christ? Actually, it now appears that the whole process of transmitting our cultural heritage is fast breaking down.

In 1920 the problem did not appear so overwhelming. At that time I was living on a Midwestern farm with my parents. Life did not seem too terribly complicated. My father taught me how to hitch up the old team of mules we had on our farmstead, how to milk a cow, and how to keep the point of a walking plow beneath the surface of the ground when plowing a furrow across a field. One day he took me into the tool shed and talked seriously to me about certain biological processes he obviously felt were important for me to understand. Having finished, he breathed a heavy sigh of relief, asked me if I thought I understood what he had been saying, and then turned away and walked out of the shed. Looking back at the incident now, I think he felt at that moment that he had completed transmitting the cultural heritage to his boy; that he had taught me the things I was going to need to know in my life. In reality, he missed the mark pretty badly. I have not hitched up a team of mules in over forty years, have milked very few cows, and have not plowed a furrow since the day he showed me how to do it.

But at that, my father did a lot better by me than I am doing by my own two sons. Recently both were attending the University. Upon listening to their conversation I frequently discovered that I did not know what they were talking about. One day I heard one boy discussing enzymatic hydroxylation. I was lost. A bit later the other boy enlarged upon anti-matter and the electron spin. I became more deeply lost.

They illustrate to me the basic problem, that while the weight and complexity of our cultural heritage have been increasing at some kind of geometric ratio no one really understands, our communication skills have simply not kept pace. What factors have caused the wide disruption between what we need to learn and our ability to learn it? By asking ourselves three questions perhaps we shall catch a glimpse of at least part of the answer.

Do we fail to devote enough time to communication?

Here, the answer is obviously no. Several studies have revealed that we devote about 70 per cent of all our waking hours to reading, writing, speaking, and listening—the four basic processes of communication.

Are our brains incapable of absorbing what we need to know? Here again the answer appears to be no. It is true, of course, that no one person can absorb all human knowledge and pass it along. The "generalists" in our culture have become fewer and fewer. But the consensus of our neurologists and physiologists is that we make very poor use indeed of the brain cells with which we are blessed. Each of us is equipped with about 11,000,000,000 brain cells, an ample supply with which to handle for many generations to come our personal needs in a pyramiding cultural heritage. The truth is that presently we are probably making effective use of less than 10 per cent of our higher mental faculties.

Are our schools failing to provide us with the kind of communication training we most need? To this question we must answer yes, and yes without too many qualifications. As a nation we read with the proficiency of a sixth-grade child; write vast numbers of memoranda with an average "fog index" so high that the meaning is lost in hopeless verbiage; listen with but 25 per cent efficiency to most of the messages we hear; and speak without confidence that we are expressing ourselves adequately or that the recipient of our words will understand what we are trying to say. Emphasis in the classroom is still too often on "correctness" rather than communication; upon form rather than upon content; upon style rather than upon understanding; upon preparation for life in a visually oriented culture as we steadily move toward a largely aurally oriented one.

Before Gutenberg man lived in essentially a speaking and listening culture. Handwritten documents became numerous, of course, after the appearance of the alphabet around 2000 B.C., but not until the printing press appeared about 500 years ago did we really build the elaborate typo-graphical culture in which we have been living. Before Gutenberg, most of what we learned was told us by parents or grandparents; most of our knowledge was stored in our minds and communicated to others through oral symbols. After Gutenberg, rapid duplication of manuscripts and documents was possible, and a widespread diffusion of ideas and knowledge could be accomplished.

It seems likely that we are now coming to the end of the Gutenberg era. Not that printed documents will no longer be produced, for we shall probably always need them. But today we are definitely drifting away from a visually oriented culture and toward an oral-aural one. Each day a new set of oral symbols somewhere replaces a former set of visual ones. The ear is quicker than the eye, more sensitive than the eye, less susceptible to impairment than the eye, and more widely perceptive than the eye. Thus, for example, oral signals are replacing visual ones in the cockpits of our jet planes. Grammar is slowly giving way to linguistics. Radio, the telephone, jet plane travel permitting face-to-face conferences, voice typewriters, tempo regulators, television and earth satellites are all giving impetus to our drift toward an aural culture. An oncoming wide variety of electronic devices insuring greater reliance upon sound and sound stimuli will soon be in common use.

Our schools are all too slow in recognizing the transformation of our culture, and in adapting their provided training to the changes taking place. Indeed, in many schools there is a complete vacuum with respect to the use of technological equipment to expedite training for improved oral communication.

THE POWER OF COMMUNICATION

The most precious possession we own is our ability to communicate. It is the main factor that has enabled man to maintain dominance over the animal world. Man alone has an ability to look at a set of data, analyze them, draw conclusions about them, and predict their likely recurrence. In this sense man makes time stand still; he gives his offspring an increment in planning time to melt the problems in their futures; he lays the groundwork for building new comforts and conveniences in an ever-improving standard of living; he transmits his cultural heritage.

Communication cannot perform this, its most basic role, unless the changing character of our culture is recognized. In the future our oral-aural media for teaching and learning are inevitably going to play larger roles. Effective communication demands a continual adaptation of our techniques, our media, and our training to our changing cultural needs. "When truth and falsehood are presented with equal skill," Aristotle once wrote, "truth will always prevail." Let us hope that the nature of truth and skill in its oral communication will be made an integral part of every school curriculum.

This book is a most important volume. It is written by a person who, because of his independent role as a professional writer, can comment freely and objectively on problems that lie essentially in the world of education. Mr. Stevens' concern for these problems has been enlarged upon in several ways. In his fifteen years as a writer he has had the opportunity of traveling widely in America. He has talked to and observed thousands of people in all walks of life. His education, writing, and public speaking have also revealed concern for our national problems, especially as they relate to communication. Today he is very much involved in the political and social life where he, his wife and four children reside. Mr. Stevens feels that one of his most important activities is serving on his local board of education, where he and his colleagues are personally involved with some of the problems discussed between these covers.

This background, I feel, has helped add to the importance of the book.

It turns out to be a very close analysis of our democratic way of life, of our dependence upon the spoken word, and of our extremely inadequate use of it. I hope that every speech and English teacher will read this book. Every training man in business and industry will find it useful. And the more tax-paying citizens who read it, the more likely will come the educational reform for which the author pleads. You will find that Mr. Stevens not only paints our communication problems with accuracy and penetration; he is also extremely explicit and thoughtful in his suggestions for seeking a solution.

Ralph G. Nichols

University of Minnesota

*The
ill-spoken
Word*

I

The Most Used, Most Important Word

IN A SMALL southern New England town passenger service along the community's railroad was all but eliminated not long ago by approval of the U.S. Interstate Commerce Commission after it held a public hearing. At the hearing, a few townspeople took the witness stand in the local courtroom to state the town's views opposing the reduction in service that had been requested by the railroad.

The speakers, obviously unprepared and unable to say what they meant, made an ineffective case for keeping the passenger service. Certainly there were reasons. People were talking about them at the coffee counters in town, but they were never clearly articulated at the hearing. The ICC in a few weeks gave its verdict in favor of the railroad.

Within a few months several public "informational" hearings were held in the same town by a dedicated committee which had studied the community's growth pattern in preparation for a forthcoming referendum on zoning. The committee wished to explain and discuss the problems of zoning which it felt was badly needed.

But in this case the hearings became a public platform for a few articulate men who attacked zoning and the committee that saw need for it. No one could orally match them. Instead of deliberation townspeople were exposed to a one-sided argument, not based on the study committee's facts but on the vocal opposition's emotion-laden generalities and suppositions. Zoning was defeated nearly two to one.

"Nobody minds too much being voted down when people have heard the facts with some semblance of truth," said a study-committee member, "but it isn't democracy at work when doubts are hammered into people's minds by the use of half truths, implications and lies. No one can say we had the facts weighed for us in this instance."

Democracy, grounded in public discussion, also suffers in the small New England village's "town meeting," the honored institution at the core of local government. Town meeting, which should truly offer an opportunity for probing the public mind, is something that most people privately defend but do not publicly attend. The town's newspaper not long ago published a photograph of an important town meeting to consider a record annual budget. Two town officials sat on the stage of the high school's 800-seat auditorium. Seven hundred and seventy of the seats were empty.

A FORGOTTEN DISCIPLINE

In this same high school, as well as in the town's primary grades, formal courses in public speaking, discussion, debate or listening are not required and oral improvement, where found at all, receives comparatively minor attention in the study of English. Nor are students likely to learn much of our heritage in the spoken word and its crucial place in a democracy. The great percentage of formal attention to the communicative uses of our language is devoted to reading. Parents, teachers, school administrators and board of education members seem determined to the point of distraction that one way or another "Johnny" must learn to read—and perhaps to do a little writing. Meanwhile, the almost totally neglected skills of speaking and listening are the ones that mainly underlie the health of the democratic action which fails so often in the New England town, as well as in the nation as a whole.

Unlike today's educators, the earliest teachers of the Western world were deeply aware of the role of speech in the lives and fortunes of men and out of this grew the study of "rhetoric," whose original meaning was concerned with the "art of expressive speech or discourse." * Now, however, it is more commonly thought of as the study of written composition. The change has come about over the decades as teachers have abandoned the study of oral language in favor of the written word.

Adherence to such a change has been supported by a false assumption. Teachers have assumed that if one learns to read and write he automatically learns to speak and listen. But this is not completely true for the spoken word represents a whole different side of language. For most people the oral side is the most important one.

To say this is not meant to diminish the written word. How people read and write is of utmost importance. It is central to thinking and learning. It is, indeed, a main key to the use of spoken language. But the written word, especially in this latter part of the twentieth century, is essentially a repository of knowledge, while spoken language becomes increasingly the word of action. It is the language tool that each of us uses every hour of the day. It is the tool for expressing thoughts that are at work immediately during their utterance. It is the tool for the give-and-take of life's endless, face-to-face discussions experienced by everyone with his fellow men. This form of communication is vastly different from the written word which lacks the personal, here-and-now quality of spoken language and is often aimed instead at an unseen audience remote in time, place and thought.

Because of the differences, it is negligent to overlook the

* It is still defined this way by Webster.

spoken word in our schools. Without it, the teaching of our mother tongue is not a complete effort. Such neglect means that we are slighting the most used, most important intellectual and verbal skills necessary to effective employment of the English language throughout a lifetime.

LEARNING TO TALK AND THINK

In the beginning of life we learn our first formal communication through language by means of the spoken word, not from teachers but mostly from the informal efforts of parents, siblings and others who talk and listen to us. This task, the learning of the mother tongue, is one of the most important in all a person's years. It not only forms the roots of his language usage, but increasing evidence indicates that it has much to do with his basic intelligence.

Thus, the quality of the spoken word that surrounds our youngest children may be a determining factor in their future. Parents with poor speech habits, reflecting the general educational neglect of the spoken word, are not likely to set exemplary basic standards for the beginning language habits of their young. Nor are they apt to establish the desirable patterns of good thinking, so integral a part of human communication. Spoken words, especially in the life's beginning years, are the grist for thought development. Indeed, this continues to be true as we grow into adulthood. At the same time speech well taught is very much involved with the relationship between good thinking aided by and reflected through good speech. Thus, when the spoken word is neglected in general education we deny parents an elemental tool for effectively carrying out their natural and crucial task of teaching their children the mother tongue, and all that goes with it.

Another such tool that goes with good speech is good listening. This skill, we have been finding, is one that can be improved through education though the teaching of it is still not well developed or accepted. It, too, is important in the early relationship between parents and children. In their efforts to express themselves and to separate reality from fantasy, the very young need good listeners. The parents who recognize this and can implement it with good listening, can stimulate the kind of self-expression which lays the proper foundations of English usage and thinking habits.

THE FAMILY CIRCLE

The spoken word continues its important role through all family life where people communicate by talking—and hardly at all by writing. The health of this communication as exercised in day-to-day relationships has a great deal to do with how well the family functions as a unit and as a most important element of society. The ability to deliberate and reach a consensus by discussion is a spoken-word skill important to the well-being of a family. It is a determining factor in everything they do. It is involved in what they buy, wear, eat, enjoy and dislike. It guides them in where they shall live, work and play. It is a part of how they shall vote, worship, argue, love, hate and educate their children. In other words, the quality of spoken discussion in a family and the quality of understanding go together. Our schools, so involved in the skills of reading and writing, do not concern themselves very much with developing the spoken-word skills of good discussion which are so central to family life.

IT'S USED ALL THE TIME

As we grow up and leave our parental home, the communication we use in everyday life is dominated by spoken language, not the written. The spoken word, largely in face-to-face conversation, becomes the most used and most important form of discourse in nearly everything we do. A number of inventories of personal communication support this contention.

One of the earliest and most noted studies was made in 1929 by Paul T. Rankin, supervising director of research and adjustment for the Detroit public schools. For two months sixty-eight adults in different occupations kept track of their communicating time by checking it every fifteen minutes of their waking hours. The data thus supplied to Dr. Rankin showed that 70 per cent of the average day was spent in some form of verbal communication. The breakdown was this: Writing, 9 per cent; reading, 16 per cent; talking, 30 per cent; and listening, 45 per cent. In the Detroit public schools at that time the greatest classroom emphasis for these four skills was placed on reading which amounted to 52 per cent. The least classroom emphasis was given to the skill most used by the average adult, listening. It received only 8 per cent of the teachers' emphasis.

Over the years other such studies have led to similar results. The spoken word for the average adult is the primary form of communication in his work. It is the basic discourse he uses in all the contacts with neighbors, friends, sales people, civic activities and public officials. It is likely to determine how the individual and his family shall vote, what he shall accept or reject in advertising and whether he shall be a leader or follower among his peers.

Added together daily speech becomes the binder for society. The quality of daily speech is a measure of the quality of society. From this standpoint, the educational imbalance between the spoken and written word found by Dr. Rankin and others is a serious consideration for all of us.

THE TECHNOLOGY OF LANGUAGE USE

The problem is compounded over and again in recent times because the importance of the spoken word has been amplified at an accelerated rate by the unprecedented speed of technological innovations. The result is a revolution in language use, chiefly with the spoken word, that is hardly recognized in much of our education. Many of our teachers are still back in the revolution of the written word brought about by developments in printing. Its rate of change, marked off in centuries, was a creeping affair compared to the one today, measured in years or even months.

From the fifteenth century when Johann Gutenberg introduced printing to the Western world the mechanical process changed little in the next four centuries, until 1810 when steam power was applied to the printing press by Friedrich Konig. It took the largest part of the 1800s before a machine was developed to set type, and create another change in the printed word. But the entire modern revolution involving spoken language has occurred in a fraction of the early eras partitioning the history of printing. Consider the telephone for example. Less than a century has passed since Alexander Graham Bell received the first telephone patent and only a half-century has gone since completion of the first transcontinental telephone line. And since 1956, which dates the first transatlantic telephone cable, under-ocean circuits have increased our overseas telephone messages nearly five times.

From 1950 to 1960 the number of U.S. telephones used in business increased by roughly 40 per cent, from 12,927,000 to 20,700,000—and nearly three million more business telephones were installed in the following three years. Since 1940 the total number of telephone conversations in the United States has more than tripled to the point where they add up to well over 100 billion per year. And telephone scientists and technicians intend that in the future their innovations will make us depend more and more on the spoken word. The time is coming when an individual may be equipped with a small vest pocket telephone that will call anywhere from any place.

True that the written word in its traditional role as the

repository of knowledge is elevated in importance by modern technical changes whose effects range from the processes of printing to the nature of libraries, but still the primary language of action is spoken, for events are happening fast in science, industry, politics and all other walks of life, and the communication woven through these events cannot wait for even the fastest written word.

SPEED DEMANDS SPOKEN WORDS

When the President of the United States is confronted with a crisis, he no longer reaches for the pen, but for the telephone or the microphone. In a few minutes he can conduct crucial affairs of state with the most important people on earth, and in another few minutes his voice can be speaking to the multitudes.

This is a nation where nearly ten of the 52 million homes equipped with television have two sets and where the average family keeps on the TV 5 hours and 25 minutes a day. Not long ago the public-school children of Des Moines, Iowa, were going to school thirty hours a week, but spending another thirty-four or thirty-five hours with television and radio. Way back in 1950 the students of that city were each reading 1.5 magazines per week, but nearly a decade later, this reading, crowded by watching and listening, was down to 0.8 magazines a week.

TRAVELING TO TALK

But not everyone is forever tied to the telephone or the TV, for ours is a nation of endless public meetings and conventions. We live in a mobile society many of whose members think little of a transcontinental flight to meet and talk with someone for a few hours. The jet airplane makes it possible for more of us to get together more often from longer distances. The automobile does the same for short distances. This all adds tremendously to the importance of the spoken word.

Some 18,000 major conventions are held in the U.S. each year and nearly 10 million people attend them. For the hotel industry, meetings and conventions make a growing, multi-billion dollar industry that runs on long-range schedules. The New York Hilton has had meetings scheduled seven years ahead of time. But in all the billion-dollar to-do, those forced to experience the conventions continually complain that the speaking is abominable and listening is practically unheard of.

William H. Whyte, Jr., an editor of *Fortune,* says, "It would be futile, of course, to hope that some cataclysm of common sense would overcome the country and put an end to speeches and conferences. We are too far gone for that, and what deep psychological needs impel us to the foolishness I cannot venture to say."

But loved or hated, used and misused, the spoken word is our primary means of human communication. It demands attention.

II

A Basic Ingredient
of Democracy

THOUGH IT GROWS in importance because of technological progress, the spoken word has always been the active language of our most important daily affairs. For example, our main democratic institutions function chiefly with oral language and their health is directly related to its quality. With this in mind, let's consider the state of the spoken word in six important areas of modern life: justice, legislation, voting, business, science and education.

1. JUSTICE

Justice as we honor it in America is a product of the spoken word and the quality of its use. To serve justice we choose juries of twelve peers to deliberate on the cases of those on trial. The twelve, according to theory, have one main channel of human communication to reach a just decision, that is by listening to testimony, the pleas of attorneys and the judge's instructions. Indeed, jurymen are not allowed to read testimony (unless certain exhibits are considered as such) while sitting at a trial. If testimony needs to be reviewed, the entire jury must *hear* it again, read aloud by the clerk of the court.

The predominance of the spoken word in exercise of the law persists to the Supreme Court where the land's last word is confined to spoken language, for the Court's proceedings are not recorded in writing. In recent years they have been tape recorded but listening to the tapes is reserved for the nine justices.

In the lower courts, where sit the citizen juries, we can be most concerned with justice and the spoken word. For one comparatively obscure, routine example, think about what happened not long ago at the Litchfield, Connecticut, Superior Court when John Hanna of nearby Danbury was tried for the murder of a local supermarket manager. Twelve jurors decided his fate after two weeks of listening to complex testimony turning upon a few pieces of circumstantial evidence. The spoken words, in transcript form, filled 3,700 typewritten pages. The judge's charge alone was a long, complexly reasoned, sometimes poetically structured discourse filled with searching questions and meanings that he hoped the twelve citizens would weigh most carefully in deciding whether the defendant went free, spent the remainder of his life in prison, or died in the electric chair. The decision was delivered against Hanna, who was sentenced to prison for life with no possible chance for pardon or parole.

THE LAWYER'S SPEAKING MATCH

Though the attorneys for Hanna's defense and the state were pretty evenly matched in speaking ability, this isn't always the case. When a serious imbalance in speech exists, the true purpose of trial by jury is sometimes badly served. A jury, of course, is impaneled in hopes the twelve will seek the truth and thereby decide upon a just course of action. But, needless to say, many a lawyer strives to win for his client rather than help the jury in its sacred duty of uncovering the truth. To do so he is likely to aim his words at swaying his listeners with oratorical mechanics not remotely concerned with the true mission of trial by jury.

James L. Jones of the Cornell University Department of Speech has pointed out that famous lawyers have often known that "winning" a verdict has meant "winning" just one member of the twelve-man jury. They have also realized, says Jones, "that since a 'jury of peers' is not selected on the basis of its logical abilities, victory could often reside in appeals to emotion and personality, rather than reasoned argument."

Speech training is not emphasized in our law schools; it is more likely to be ignored, or limited to no more than coaching individuals who badly need help. But practicing attorneys soon discover that courtroom success depends very much on the ability to be orally articulate. Some lawyers then train themselves or seek outside help.

One day in a Manhattan court, New York City's Assistant District Attorney Maurice Nadjari made what a *New York Times* reporter called a "high-decibel oration." "His phrases . . . quickly awakened all those on the benches who had been lulled by the mumbling between judges, lawyers and witnesses before the appearance of Mr. Nadjari," said the reporter, who then proceeded to investigate where the highly articulate lawyer had come by his skill. The answer was puzzling. "In spite of his forensic fury," said the *Times* writer, "Mr. Nadjari didn't train either in oratory or debate at any of the schools he attended—DeWitt Clinton High School, City College or New York University Law School."

Lack of formal speech education for law students results in general unevenness of oral ability to persuade the nation's juries. This can hardly serve that central pillar of justice, the seeking of truth. The man with the best techniques of tongue can all too frequently lead jurors around the truth to win a guilty client's case, while his opponent, less able to move the twelve peers, loses along with the side of truth. The nation's attorneys with silver tongues, of course, demand the highest fees. Here we find one good reason why the rich man has a better chance to win his case than a poor client.

THE LISTENING JURORS

Besides the omission of speech in law schools, justice by jury is hardly served by general education. American jury members have seldom been taught the most elemental principles of oral persuasion, therefore, they have little or no working knowledge of what happens before them in court. Also their schooling has done little to develop critical listening, the skill a juryman obviously needs above all else. Such ill prepared jurors naturally get caught up by *how* testimony is presented and miss *what* is being directed at them.

In the Connecticut case of John Hanna, where the jurors heard nearly 8 million words, an informal survey following the trial revealed that none of the twelve had ever received a moment's planned training in the skill of listening. Most expressed surprise that courses in listening improvement are taught, that the fleeting act of comprehending, retaining and critically analyzing what we hear is a definite, unique skill that can be improved through teaching. Nor could the jurors say they had ever received the kind of rhetorical training which might have helped them recognize and analyze the oral proof presented for and against Hanna.

DECISIONS BEHIND DOORS

Finally we might think of the decision-making process which engaged the American jury as it reaches a verdict requiring that twelve people, frequently strangers from various walks of life, enter into a discussion which must be well conducted if justice is to be served. But good discussion is by no means one of our notable traits, nor is it a skill that American education helps develop very much. Too frequently one of a group, a person vocally (but not mentally) superior, "wins" the discussion and thereby prevents arrival at a true consensus. When this happens in the jury room, the cause of truth is unlikely to be served.

2. LEGISLATION

The Federal and state legislative branches of government certainly revolve around the spoken word, for much of the information gathering and the generation of legislative ideas comes from "hearings," followed by legislative decisions which are supposedly made through public discussion and debate. But are these spoken tools in good order? The answer is "no!"

The United States Congress is now seldom, if ever, the scene of what one can truly call debate, even though our Senators and Congressmen would appear to be forever talking, according to the *Congressional Record*. The "talk" of the eighty-seventh Congress, for example, hit an all-time peak by filling 42,496 pages of the *Record*, but close examination reveals that the sound of this so-called talk frequently does not cross the floors of Congress. The *Record* is a printed compilation of insertions ranging from constituents' letters, to articles, to speeches made outside the Congress and speeches prepared for delivery there, but never uttered anywhere.

The abandon of all this "talk" was illustrated by the then Senator Barry Goldwater when the *Congressional Record* carried a speech labeled as his and entitled "Is Conservatism Dynamic?" The Senator was said to have given the speech in Montclair, New Jersey, but soon his staff said the insertion was a clerical error, that the Senator had not made any speech in Montclair. The one in the *Congressional Record*, actually a talk critical of the Arizona lawmaker, had been given by a Princeton University scholar.

In another case a strange coincidence involved two Coloradoans each of whom made a speech on the same day praising an airline in their state. One, a congressman, supposedly uttered his speech in the House of Representatives, while the other, a senator, was recorded as having spoken in the Senate. The oratorical efforts were the same, word-for-word.

TALK WITHOUT LISTENERS

Speech of course is exercised on the floors of Congress but to the dismay of visitors who watch and listen from the galleries, the spectacle is often that of one lonely speaker with no one listening, or pretending to listen. Even "priority" measures receive such slipshod attention. When the $1.1 billion Appalachia bill, which at the time headed the President's "top priority" legislative list, came before the Senate, only nine members of the great deliberative body were on hand to hear a flurry of criticism that was reported as the "opening of debate."

Most of our legislative orators have lost listeners because their mundane material often serves only some minor, petty interest traceable to the speaker's vote-getting efforts, or worse than that, to a legislative lobby. One of the most flagrant examples is that of a Maryland representative who was sentenced in 1963 to six months in prison and a $5,000 fine for accepting money for making a speech on the House floor defending the operations of independent savings and loans associations. The conviction, said the U.S. Department of Justice, "affects public confidence in the integrity of congressional debate."

A PRACTICE OF THE PAST

The public, however, appears to know little about debate, which slips into the past of the United States Congress.

The lack of issues is not the cause; history's greatest problems are before today's elected representatives, but generally these issues have not even been lightly warmed by the forge of true debate.

Disarmament is one of those great issues but as the federal military budget has annually reached the houses of Congress, it passes with hardly a mild query. One recent defense appropriation bill of $47 billion was briefly considered before the House of Representatives with only one feeble dissent when Missouri's Representative Thomas B. Curtis questioned whether or not the United States had the money for such an expenditure. He and his colleagues said nothing of some truly important moral and political questions of defense spending. The following day John G. Norris of the *Washington Post* wrote: "Yesterday's debate on the big spending bill, which lasted less than three hours, was largely a dull performance. Much time was consumed by members from government and private shipyard areas arguing how much naval ship-building and repair funds should go to each."

John Crosby, the *New York Herald Tribune* columnist, commented, "The word debate is not easy to define, and that makes it hard to pinpoint when the last serious debate occurred on the Senate floor. Some congressional observers feel the last real debate on foreign policy was over NATO, the so-called troops-to-Europe issue in 1949. The last debate anyone remembers where oratory actually changed votes was over the censure of Senator Joseph McCarthy. . . ."

SECRECY, SENIORITY AND SCIENCE

One major deterrent to the congressional debate of great modern issues has been the growth of official secrecy applied in the name of national security. Though much of the secrecy has been proven ridiculous, as well as harmful to the true needs of national security, its over exercise by the executive branch of the government has been contagious, and a curtain of covertness has often hidden what should be open discussion and debate in the legislative branch. In this great arm of government which should of all places be a model of open discussion, 38 per cent of all committee sessions are closed.

Minnesota's Senator Eugene McCarthy had this to say about the inroads of secrecy: "You find the Administration saying: 'If you knew what we know, you wouldn't hold the point of view you do.' How can you argue against that? Many of the great issues confronting Congress are wrapped in official secrecy so that congressmen can hardly argue against them, or they are so complicated that no one but scientists can understand them. Or both."

The founding fathers, as they wrote our Constitution, said nothing to foster secrecy, but they were outspokenly in favor of free and open discussion. At mid-twentieth century, however, fear-generating secrecy often squelches the open debate which few can deny is a cornerstone of our democracy. "When debate moves out of sight," concluded John Crosby in a series of columns about Congress, "a good deal of high principle, without which the country can't be decently governed, is lost."

Another deterrent to open debate is the organization of the Congress itself which prevents us from hearing our duly elected senators and congressmen speak out on important issues. The congressional seniority system allows the domination of many congressional committees by senators and representatives who long ago forgot their responsibilities to the principles of free and open deliberation. A leading example of how public debate can be stifled is found in the King-Anderson Bill, to provide "Medicare" for nearly 19 million elderly Americans. For eight years the Medicare bill was not fully or freely debated because it was prevented from leaving a House committee dominated by one man. If our citizens understood the crucial nature of debate to good government, such undemocratic procedure could not endure the public censure it would receive.

A third deterrent to congressional debate of modern issues is the one cited by Senator Eugene McCarthy when he says that many problems are so complicated that no one but scientists can understand them. The Senator might have added that a great many scientists seem unable to prevent this difficulty because of their inability to communicate with anyone but themselves. This applies to the written word and definitely to the spoken medium which, with its give-and-take facility for developing understanding, is crucial for communication between a scientific and a lay mind. But those studying the problems of science communication in recent years have discovered that the typical scientist, despite his extensive education, has seldom developed the ability to speak his own language well.

A case in point is a routine meeting that I observed in Washington one morning when the U.S. Patent Office was seeking some $3 million to develop a special information retrieval system to speed up and simplify patent searches. Two scientists tried to explain the system to staff members of the Bureau of the Budget and a House congressional committee staff, but within minutes the first scientist lost his listeners, though he didn't sense the loss. During a coffee break most of the small audience left—and just as well, for the program's second half was equally uncommunicative. The appropriation was approved, but the action, if taken intelligently, could not have been based on the abortive meeting.

Such performances undoubtedly contribute to the lack of debate on many pressing and momentous problems that require even minor understanding of science and technology. Little in the nature of a valid congressional debate has been conducted, for example, about the priorities we should assign to the nation's large, ultra-expensive science projects. Should we go to the moon while men suffer on earth from heart disease and cancer? Or should we develop a supersonic airliner while America's badly needed train service has had no new, basic technological improvements since last century?

The State Legislator's Image

The disarray of what passes for public discussion and debate is not limited to the nation's highest legislative bodies, as was evident when 500 state lawmakers from across the nation met in Boston to consider a topic entitled: "Improving the Public Image of the State Legislator." The solons generally agreed that their "image" was bad. Some well-known political writers and editors were also at the meeting to add their thoughts. The crumpled image, as it was discussed, again reflected the misuse of speech in high places.

For instance, Earl C. Behrens, political editor of the *San Francisco Chronicle,* said the trouble is traceable directly to the questionable conduct of the lawmakers themselves. Behrens paraphrased Shakespeare, saying that "all legislative chambers are a stage upon which each member plays a part. The manner in which you play your part creates your image." And that image for many state lawmakers, said the San Francisco editor, is developed from "disgraceful decorum in the chambers, clownish vulgarity . . . of house jesters, and the garrulous lawmaker who thinks he is knowledgeable but is not." Many of the visiting solons agreed.

Here is what can happen with the low state of debate in our legislatures: Not many months before the Boston conference, three amendments to the United States Constitution were quietly put before the nation's state legislatures. The amendments, in the words of *The New York Times,* "would upset the whole structure of federal-state relations and establish a veto over the Supreme Court. . . ." Within a short time, many state legislatures had approved the constitutional amendments. They were on the way to passage. But then

President John F. Kennedy and other critics, like New Jersey's Governor Richard J. Hughes and Senator Clifford P. Case, warned the nation's solons of the amendments' potential dangers. This stopped what might have come close to automatic acceptance of the questionable measures.

"They [the amendments] marched through one state legislature after another without debate or consideration of their destructive potentialities," said the *Times*. "The disturbing question that remains . . . is how such proposals could be swept through so easily in the first place, especially in a state like New Jersey. How many other harmful bills slip into law before anyone bothers to consider their implications?"

3. THE VOTING DECISION

In 1860 the winning candidate for the Presidency, Abraham Lincoln, made no formal campaign speeches between his nomination and election. In 1960 the winning candidate, John F. Kennedy, made over 400 speeches between nomination and election, and an untold additional number in the preceding primaries. His talks, given under all kinds of circumstances, from shopping centers and hotel lobbies to America's largest auditoriums, reached audiences of a dozen or less and others so large they are incomprehensible. The campaign speeches of President Kennedy were printed by the U.S. Senate Subcommittee on Freedom of Communications; they required nearly a thousand pages of fine, closely spaced print. A comparable number of pages were needed for Vice President Nixon's speeches.

The documents do not include the so-called Great Debates of 1960, which were printed in a third subcommittee book. The debates found the largest audiences ever to hear any kind of political discourse. Estimates say that those who heard all the debates ranged in numbers from 85 million

(Dr. George Gallup) to 120 million (The Columbia Broadcasting System). A nationwide survey by Dr. Elmo Roper indicated that 57 per cent of the 1960 voters were influenced in their decisions by the debates. Six per cent, or over 4 million, said they based their voting decisions on the debates alone. Of this number nearly 3 million gave their vote to President Kennedy, which by itself was enough to win for him, when we recall that he led by only 112,000 votes.

ELECTRONICS AND POLITICS

With the coming of radio, and especially its use by Franklin Delano Roosevelt, the spoken word moved to the front of the American voting decision. In 1940 a Columbia University group made an intensive survey of how people formed their opinions for voting in that year's Roosevelt-Willkie campaign. The investigators, using Erie County, Pennsylvania, as a laboratory, visited every fourth house to interview some 3,000 people once a month from May to November. To make up their minds for voting, the great majority of people said that the radio was their "most important" source of information.

"The listener gets a sense of personal access from the radio which is absent from print," commented the researchers. "Politics on the air more readily becomes an active experience ... closer to a personal relationship."

The Erie study also revealed another powerful factor in election campaigns. Defined as "personal influence," it, too, very much involved spoken language, for it took into account all the talk that goes on between people in an election. Personal influence, the Columbia study found, was an important opinion source for the voting decision. In fact, it was discovered that the people whose ideas changed most during the 1940 campaign claimed they were altered after talking to friends, discussing politics at work, because of family discussions, and even as the result of overhearing political statements in a public place.

Another such study, made of the 1948 Presidential election in Elmira, New York, again revealed the campaign's oral side played a predominant role in voting decisions. The researchers were concerned with how people perceived the election and their findings were not flattering to the speaking and listening habits of Americans. It was shown that the typical voter is likely to accept what he hears only if it is favorable to his point of view, and he rejects or distorts that which is unfavorable.

FRESH POLITICAL AIR

With the growth of television, audiences and voter interest in national political campaigns grew tremendously. The 1960 Kennedy-Nixon debates seemed to be the beginning of a new and much welcomed change in campaigning. While they really were not debates or oral encounters of substance and high quality, they came as fresh air compared to the stale political diatribes that we as Americans know only too well. There for short periods stood the candidates, face-to-face, attempting to discuss the campaign issues, rather than wracking body and mind crisscrossing the nation with a troop of ghost writers who alter a standard speech to fit this or that occasion or place.

The Great Debates, to many political observers, looked like the beginning of saner election campaigns. Walter Lippman considered them "a bold innovation which is bound to be carried forward into future campaigns and could not now be abandoned." The president of the Columbia Broadcasting System, Dr. Frank Stanton, said, "The great unfinished business of the Constitution remains to assure a more informed electorate. In 1960 we found an answer in a sound and constructive use of electronic communications." Newton N. Minow, who became chairman of the Federal Communication Commission in the Kennedy Administration, said: "One need not be a scholar to perceive that the Great Debates of the 1960 Presidential campaign constituted an event of monumental significance in the history of our Constitution."

STALENESS AGAIN

But in the 1964 election the candidates did not debate. In sharp, disheartening contrast the campaign was among history's prime examples of how speech should not be used by a democracy to choose a leader. The audiences—and again with radio and television they were huge—heard the Republican candidate Barry Goldwater continually attack the character of the Democratic candidate, President Lyndon B. Johnson, who, in the face of all that he was called, obviously decided to hold his tongue. The Goldwater attacks neither revealed what the Arizonan had in mind for conducting the nation's affairs, nor did they cause the incumbent President to explain and defend his current and future programs. The people who thought of the 1960 debates as the seeds of improvement, turned in disgust from the 1964 spectacle.

Walter Lippman, a week before election day, wrote: "If all that mattered were the outcome of the election, we might pay little further attention to the whole ugly business which has dragged this election down to the lowest level within memory. But there is more than the election at stake. The office of the President of the United States has been treated with utter vulgar disrespect. The character of the man who will continue to be President of the United States has been maligned by his rival in a manner which has hitherto been reserved for anonymous inciters of whispering campaigns." Mr. Lippman concluded that column by saying: "I think I shall now wash my hands. But I should like to say that I look forward to next week when I expect to have the delicious feeling that comes with no longer having a toothache."

The 1964 voter, said a number of political writers, was puzzled and disgusted by the year's Presidential politics, and they hoped an irate citizenry would demand future improvement. But to do so, the voter needs an understanding of the standards he should demand if voting campaigns are to serve our democratic ideals. He obviously lacks such understanding and one large reason is that his education does not introduce him to the important areas of good discussion and debate on which sensible campaigns will have to depend.

"The art of public speaking and the field of politics have been bound together since the beginning of time," said David L. Lawrence, former Governor of Pennsylvania. "Far more important, the evolution of free public speech in an open forum gave birth to democracy and, in the last analysis, liberated mankind."

4. BUSINESS

In American business and industry the spoken word has received considerable attention since World War II. For that matter industrial managers have talked so much about "oral communication" that it is now an office cliché, but major changes in the business structure have forced leaders to concern themselves deeply with how people understand one another. Over and again they have found that the main substance of communication in industry is what two speech educators, Harold P. Zelko and Harold J. O'Brien, called the "oral, face-to-face relationship."

"Communication looms ever larger in total management planning," say Zelko and O'Brien, as they explain why the oral medium has become important to business. "American industry is undergoing a revolution today which places an even greater emphasis on people than yesterday's industrial revolution placed on machines. The present goals of industrial management are teamwork, cooperation and great enough participation to make all employees feel a part of the social work-group. Communication has reached a major position in achievement of these goals. To comprehend the part it plays management must understand the total communication process—all channels and mediums possible for improving the internal and external communication of the organizations. . . ."

MANAGERS NEED GOOD SPEECH

The overall communication methods of business have been inventoried by many investigators who invariably find the spoken word the primary medium—despite the fact that business wallows in paperwork. For example, the Communication Research Staff of Purdue University questioned the presidents of America's one hundred largest corporations about the communication needs of their industries. Those answering showed a decided preference for oral methods of business communication. Ninety-eight per cent said that oral communication was at least as important as written, and 40 per cent said it was more important. The great majority of respondents felt that the effectiveness of people in management is directly related to their effectiveness with spoken language.

This is true at all levels, from foremen and supervisors to top management people, who, according to the University of Michigan Research Center for Group Dynamics, spend one-fourth to one-half of their lives in meetings. But as people enter business they arrive unequipped with adequate speaking and listening skills. One authoritative estimate, reported in *The New York Times,* said that within the one hundred top American corporations some $250 million a year of expensive executive time is lost through unnecessary, poorly planned and badly conducted meetings. For many years American management has been trying through adult education to remedy such failings of the spoken word inherited from general education.

CONCERN FOR IMPROVEMENT

The first efforts at oral improvement in business were usually through public-speaking courses which seemed to fit management's methods of a few decades ago—described by Harold P. Zelko of Pennsylvania State University as the "more directive, authoritarian and boss tactics of the past." But the philosophy has changed, and though public speaking is still a popular course, the best of industrial training makes it only a segment of a diversified approach to oral communication.

"We now find the goals of progressive management to include the development of leadership, participation and group activity," says Dr. Zelko. "We see the concern for developing a 'social climate' and an atmosphere of 'permissiveness' within the organization and within the work groups. It was inevitable that to do this managers must be more skilled as communicators, and particularly in the abilities for talking things over informally and for leading and participating in meetings and conferences. More delegation, counseling and consultation practices bring a greater need for interviewing and counseling skills. Performance ratings and evaluations of both subordinates and executives also emphasize this need. Whereas a deficient employee of the past was alternately 'bawled out,' criticized or even fired by his superior, today's manager sits down and counsels him. As managers found that they could profitably draw on their subordinates for advice and participation in solving problems, a need developed for greater ability in the skill of listening."

In management's attempt to improve oral communication, the training has varied from high-quality university-level instruction down to gimmickery vended by people ill qualified for teaching skills of spoken language. The same variation in quality applies to the extensive how-to literature in use. However, the surveys of business communication, conducted by universities like Purdue, and organizations like the National Industrial Conference Board, indicate that serious training in oral skills is gaining headway, under courses of instruction described variously as oral communication, conference leadership, group discussion, listening, interviewing and counseling.

5. SCIENCE

Scientific communication quite naturally leads one to think of written words, for the image is that of a smocked scientist working quietly in his laboratory consulting "the literature" as he prepares his experiments, then writing down his procedures and results to be used when this work is published—and on and on. "Publish or Perish," has for ages been a motto of scientists whose stock in trade is the technical literature. But while the old image still remains, the focus changes considerably.

In Cleveland, the Case Institute of Technology made a survey to learn what scientists do and the results were surprising. "Contrary to the stereotype of a chemist as a quiet smocked man in a laboratory bending over a rack of test tubes," said the study's report, "the average chemist seems to spend more time in scientific communication than in all the rest of his professional activities combined."

Of the working hours surveyed the average chemist spent 2.5 hours thinking and planning, 3.0 hours in data treatment, 10.4 hours with his equipment and 23.2 hours in scientific and business communication. Of the communication time, by far the greatest percentage was oral, with talking used by

each individual much more than any other medium of communication. A comparatively small percentage of the time
was spent reading and about half of that was used absorbing
general information rather than material specifically related
to the task at hand.

WRITTEN WORDS TOO SLOW

While "publication" has been the traditional means of
conveying scientific information, the rapidly changing nature of science in recent years has also been changing the
modes of communication, as indicated by the well publicized
"information explosion." New findings and technical planning of a year ago, or less, are old or even obsolescent today.
At this fast pace, the written word has difficulty keeping up
with what is happening. Scientists the world over are concerned that while scientific material is increasing by the ton,
its slowness in reaching the right people at the right time is
an increasing problem. Oral language is often the answer.

"One method of information processing is the fastest and
cheapest of all," writes Walter Sullivan, *The New York
Times* science editor. "This is the spoken word. No matter
how elaborate automatic systems may become, they probably
will never replace the formal conference or the informal 'bull
session.' "

In today's rapidly evolving world of science, the frontiers
of many disciplines are carried strictly by spoken language
because of the slow pace of written language. It has been au-
thoritatively estimated that the written word in many cases
lags behind the true state of an art, as reflected by what scientists are talking about, by as much as a year or two. The lag
may be even greater in some disciplines.*

---

* From a private conversation with Joshua Stern of the National Bureau
of Standards.

POORLY SPOKEN SCIENCE

In science, as elsewhere, those concerned with communication find that though the spoken word is a primary medium the lack of oral skills prevents it working most effectively. Recently the President's Science Advisory Committee made a report on the problems of scientific information in which the seventeen-man panel drew attention "to the importance of good communication to modern scientific and technical endeavor." The committee delved into the processes of communication and explored possible techniques, such as journalistic methods, for improving science information. But the committee concluded that the entire problem is difficult to solve without improving the very basic skills of clear expression.

"Much more obvious than any deficiency in our understanding of the communication process itself," said the committee's report, "is our inability to use natural English properly. This panel is gravely concerned, as are many others who have written on the information problem, that so many American scientists and technologists can neither speak nor write effective English, that the new language of science and technology is turgid, heavy and unclear. This is a problem that goes beyond what the Panel has set out to do. The seeds of articulateness are sown in the home and at the elementary and high-school level. . . ."

The quantity and quality of the spoken word affects science at all levels because the modern scientist no longer works alone, but usually as a member of a well-staffed laboratory, generously equipped with telephones to keep its researchers in close touch with a wide circle of fellow scientists. Such research centers, of course, have numerous formal meetings among their staffs, but they also have untold numbers of routine, unplanned get togethers that are fostered because of their importance to the fertilization of scientific thinking. It is recognized that when a group of scientists loses its chance to talk freely and informally, the productivity of ideas is likely to suffer.

The spoken word is also a main ingredient of all the regional, national and international conferences which have traditionally been the backbone of formal scientific communication. Here is where the scientist brings the fruit of his work in the form of technical papers that are read aloud to the conferees. As a scientist completes his reading he then finds himself in a "crucible of criticism," where his work is orally discussed by the people of his discipline, including the top authorities in the field. According to what happens in the discussion the paper is published in a journal, presented again after being changed by new thinking or new work, or rejected completely. The crucible of criticism, very much a product of the spoken word, has been the quality control system of science.

But the system is not working well. In the first place, many scientific conferences are so large that the processes of criticism couldn't possibly work. At Atlantic City not long ago, the Federation of American Societies for Experimental Biology met and in a few days 3,138 papers were presented. To crowd them all into the schedule at times required thirty-four simultaneous sessions. At many such sessions, where scientists unskilled at oral interpretation read their papers aloud, few people listen. Not only is the articulation of such papers bad, but so is the content which, of course, is central to the information system.

In *Science,* the magazine of the American Association for the Advancement of Science, Phillip H. Abelson, the editor, wrote an editorial about the difficulties: "Instead of tackling these communication problems we have ignored them, and we have retrogressed, for we have allowed our standards to deteriorate. We permit and even encourage scientists to deliver virtually the same lecture at meeting after meeting. It is annoying and wasteful to make a special effort to hear a paper only to find that the speaker is repeating, almost verbatim, material he has presented earlier."

THE LOST WORDS

But scientists attend conferences more than ever, and many of them find the trips worthwhile—not solely because of the traditional paper reading and critical procedures, but because of a widely developed informal system of face-to-face conferences. While the official system proceeds, the conferees seek each other out in the halls, hotel rooms, restaurants and bars, where one finds in informal sessions some of the most important communication of science today. Here is where much of the cross-fertilization of ideas so important to modern science is most likely to occur. Such communication, of course, may never reach the printed word, which is a serious matter for the perpetuation of science from generation to generation.

"The loss of information at today's scientific meetings must be tremendous," says Raymond A. Jensen, Executive Secretary of the National Federation of Science Abstracting and Indexing Services. "We all know that a large amount of what is said at the conferences is simply bantered around the meeting halls and hotels. Furthermore there is little doubt but this is the most advanced material in today's science."

MORE MEANINGFUL SPOKEN SCIENCE

Improvements in scientific conferences, if made, are likely to relate to the more skillful and better planned use of spoken language. The formal side of scientific meetings needs attention to find ways of making the oral presentations and criticisms of scientific findings more effective. Also, communication studies should seek ways for making the informal sessions more meaningful and useful to science in general.

Science consists of man learning to converse with nature. Nature, who is always right in her statements, is free and willing to talk to all men, though she often is difficult to comprehend. Thus, it stands to reason that science can profit if all men can improve their skills for conducting clear discourse so they may better draw upon one another's observations, and thereby help illuminate the complex relationships of nature. To use words well, especially in the oral medium, is not only important to science, it is crucial.

6. EDUCATION

Good speech and good teaching are inseparable, for the teacher, regardless of curriculum content, employs spoken language as the primary tool of his trade. The teacher, of course, needs many unique personal and intellectual qualities to teach and inspire his students, but with them all he can fail if he lacks ability to speak and listen well. Furthermore, the teacher, regardless of curriculum content, is a speech teacher, like it or not, for how he speaks, listens and generally treats the spoken word in his classroom has a direct bearing on his students' oral language abilities.

These concepts are not seriously questioned, but they have been badly overlooked by the educators of the nation's teachers. For the past couple of decades, numerous studies have revealed that attention to spoken language was inadequate. For example:

A Stanford University study completed in 1944 indicated that over half (51 per cent) of 1,200 prospective teachers were ill-prepared in six basic speech skills. At about the same time, a survey of six Minnesota teachers colleges turned up comparable results.

Nearly a decade later the speech needs of Texas public-school teachers were the subject of a study by Crannell Tolliver who concluded: "Though, the literature [about teacher training] stresses the importance of good speech on the part of teachers, the data collected indicates that to the administrators, teacher-placement agencies, etc., the speech of teachers is not very important." Tolliver found: (1) a general weakness in speech training programs for prospective teachers; (2) a general lack of consistency in the speech courses that are offered; (3) indications that the right kinds of speech courses for teachers are not offered at all; (4) that teachers, who are especially weak in the much needed classroom skill of oral reading, receive no helpful work with it in their training; and (5) a generally unsatisfactory program to screen prospective teachers for speech inadequacy.

A 1961 report of the National Council of Teachers of English revealed that more than a third (37.5 per cent) of the teacher colleges do not give a course in speech to prospective elementary English teachers. Worse still, when one considers how important is the oral reading of literature in the early years of school, only 17.5 per cent of these institutions give a course in oral interpretation to the English majors who are later charged with making literature an exciting experience for the nation's elementary students. If anyone should be concerned in school about the development of good speech habits, it should be the English teacher.

In 1962 Marceline Erickson of Mankato State Teachers College in Minnesota completed a survey of catalogues from 339 central states' colleges and universities to ascertain what they offered for the speech improvement of future secondary-school teachers. Less than a third (31 per cent) required a course in basic voice and speech improvement; less than half (43 per cent) required a course in public speaking, discussion and debate, and barely a third (34 per cent) required a course in oral interpretation, the skill so important to teachers who continually read aloud to students.

A Basic Thread

Those taking a close look at speech as an educator's tool often feel that with proper attention to the spoken word in teacher-training institutions, speech might serve as a basic thread for educational methods courses which as they now exist have been described as suffering "from a high degree of dullness and superfluity," and as a type of training "where the student never seems to exercise his right to expect stimulation." A look at these courses, which are under attack from many quarters, reveals that if speech is at all considered in some 120 semester hours of teacher training it amounts to no more than two or three hours of the "fundamentals of speech" or "public speaking." But such a bare minimum of oral training can hardly be expected to help the teacher with the spoken-word skills he will continually need.

In an extensive dissertation on speech and teaching completed at Columbia University's Teachers College, Burton H. Byers commented on the inadequate oral training of teachers. "Most teachers colleges," he said, "do not provide a program which brings into clear focus the relationships between speaking-listening customs and competencies and the basic democratic values. Without such focus, students learn about democracy without learning to identify demagoguery, or how demagoguery relates to democratic values, or how to counteract it.

"Most teachers colleges lack programs for bringing into clear focus the pedagogical uses of speech techniques: oral questioning, extemporizing explanations, oral reading and discussion.

"Most teachers colleges fail to provide practice in the use

of speaking-listening techniques in real or simulated class-room situations. Courses in speech, as well as courses in writing and literature, are notably lacking in this vital class-room activity. Student-teaching experiences cannot be made to compensate for the failure of courses in speech and English to provide the necessary professionalized experiences in speaking-listening."

THE TEACHER'S POOR SPEECH

That the teachers of teachers do not recognize the speech needs of their profession is often evident in their own lack of oral skills. One observer, James D. Koerner, who visited about 200 teacher-training classes in colleges and universities, describes what he saw in his book *The Miseducation of American Teachers*. The would-be listeners, he says, "gaze around the room, squirm in their seats, doze and watch the clock." Attempts to start discussions are met with "no response." Students do not volunteer nor challenge statements. And if a discussion does commence it proceeds at a low level and sel-dom goes anywhere.

Here is Dr. Koerner's description of a lecture by an Ed.D. of educational psychology on the subject of Comenius, the seventeenth-century Czech educator who advocated relating education to everyday life. "The instructor lectures from note cards. He has an extremely poor carrying voice and focuses his eyes on the far corner of the room at the ceiling, staring there throughout the class. 'Colmenius,' he says, 'was a sense realist. You know what that is.' No response from the class. 'A sense realist,' he says, reading from a card, 'is one who believes in the evidence of his senses only. But Comenius was also very religious.' He drones along for the remainder of the period, during which no student says anything, reading data about Comenius's life and what he takes to be Comenius's 'philosophy.' He succeeds in making the generous

Moravian a thoroughly dry and unattractive character ...
Perhaps it doesn't matter: the class is singularly uninterested
in the proceedings; some students talk with one another
while the instructor reads from his cards; some read magazines; some are preoccupied with their attire, their lipstick,
or their tennis shoes; and some few, bent closely over their
desks, furiously scribble in their notebooks, apparently trying
to record the lecture verbatim."

A SPEECH CHAIN

Those who have delved into the matter of listening know
that *good speech habits beget good speech habits.* If this
axiom works, it certainly demands that we improve the learning chain of spoken language from the teacher's teacher, to
the teacher, to the student. It is also an elementary fact that
except for the need to talk with and listen to students, teachers and their schools could be replaced solely with textbooks.
No excuse can say that spoken-language improvement should
not be a primary concern of teacher training. Two decades
ago in England it was decided:

"(a) that the Board of Education should require every
[teacher] training institution to pay attention to the speech
of every student, and every area training authority to include
in the assessment of a student's practical teaching his ability
to use the English language. . . ." The report, including this
statement, said that poor speech was one of the problems behind what was considered a failure of education in England.
With particular reference to speech, the report said: "English
is everyone's business, and a teacher no matter what his subject, who is not incidentally training his pupils in a mastery
of the English language is a failure."

III

The Precious Jewel
of the Brain

MAN OF COURSE talked long before he wrote. It is also true that in all of his time on earth man has talked far more than he has written. Of all languages used on earth few have ever been converted from their original spoken form to a written form. One authoritative estimate places the figure at "no more than five per cent."

This primacy of speech in the development of civilized man seems to have endowed him with a brain and allied mechanisms designed chiefly for formal-language communication with the spoken word. This design, it would seem, should be carefully considered in educating anyone to use his own language. But educators, in their devotion to the written word, seem to have forgotten that in the area of language, man was primarily developed as a talker and listener. The common emphasis today might lead to the false conclusion that man was first and foremost a reader and writer.

The first formal symbolized communication of any civilization has been oral, long before the written word was conceived. The British biologist J. Z. Young points out the earliest signs of civilization reveal that "the cement for the formation of societies" has been the human drive for men to assemble and communicate. Throughout the world, from the beginnings of civilization, there is evidence of people gathering in crowds, usually for the overt purpose of witnessing great events, but for the basic underlying purpose of conversing with one another. At first they assembled on the sides of suitably shaped hills. Then artificial hills, still visible in many places on earth, were built to serve the need for men to meet and talk. "In no other animal," says Professor Young, "is the habit of assembly quite so well developed as it is in man. The biological significance of the habit is that by it the brain associations necessary for communication are formed."

Likewise, in no other animal do we find the distinctly human capability of communication by speech. Suzanne K. Langer, Professor of Philosophy at Connecticut College, put it this way: "The great step from anthropoid to anthropos, animal to man, was taken when the vocal organs were moved to register the occurrence of an image, and stirred an equivalent occurrence in another brain, and the two creatures referred to the same thing.

"To evoke ideas in each other's minds, not in the course of action, but of emotion and memory—that is, in reflection— is to communicate *about* something; and that is what no animals do."

A PLACE IN THE BRAIN

How did man come by this unique ability? The mechanisms behind it were not understood until the middle of the last century when a French surgeon, Paul Broca, did his postmortem brain studies of people who had exhibited speech defects before death. One of Broca's notable contributions to neurology was that of showing how cerebral damage related to speech revealed that specific parts of the brain provided man with his speech capability. Neurological investigation then slowly pieced together how particular brain areas, not found in animals, are the links between man's mind and his language.

This knowledge, increased immensely by recent research, indicates that speech has the primary role in communication. The primacy is particularly emphasized by neurological evidence that practically all human communication—including the written form and certain nonverbal forms such as gestures—is neurologically funneled through the cerebral mechanisms responsible for connecting thought and speech.

Anyone interested in the neurological importance of speech will definitely learn of Wilder Penfield, a scientist and neurosurgeon who heads the Montreal Neurological Institute of McGill University. Dr. Penfield and his associates have spent many years mapping the human cortex, the convoluted outer surface of the brain.

This investigative work is a necessary by-product of brain surgery for focal epilepsy. Each patient remains conscious and alert while a "trap door" is surgically cut into a locally anesthetized part of the skull to expose a chosen area of the cortex—which, incidentally, lacks sensory connections and therefore has no feeling or sense of pain. The cortex in view, the investigators gently touch it with probes that are ever so mildly electrified. As the electric stimulation of the brain takes place, the patient's reactions are observed and even discussed with him. For example, if the trap door on one patient leads to a portion of the cortex related to vision, an electric probe may cause him to see strange flashes of light. From these reactions the brain scientists have been able to "map" the varied and complex functions of the human cortex. Most fascinating to Dr. Penfield has been the brain's role in speech, a subject on which he and an associate, Lamar Roberts, have written an important book.

The neurologists show us that if the brain areas related to human motor (muscular) control could be spread out like a map, the two largest provinces would be those tied to the use of the hands and to the process of vocalization. The latter province is equipped for the deft mechanical control of the lips, jaw, tongue and face. By electrically stimulating this part of the brain, the Montreal scientists have been able to block or distort speech (but not produce it, as some might think). A patient experiencing the blockage could think of a word, but then find himself unable to sound it out, or if he could, the term might be badly distorted. This result, the investigators knew, was not much different from what would happen if you clamped your hand over a person's mouth, shutting off or at least distorting his speech. No one could say that in the attempt to speak a word, it had not reached the tongue, for it had been thought of and mentally made ready for articulation, though the actual vocalization was prevented.

But this kind of speech interception did not answer the most important question of all: Where and how does thought become a word ready for action by the lips, tongue, face and throat. Dr. Penfield and fellow scientists have found the "where" of the question, but the "how" touches the deepest mysteries of the brain.

THE GATE BETWEEN THOUGHT AND WORD

By their ingenious mapping methods the scientists have delineated three cortical speech areas, normally located on the brain's left hemisphere and somehow involved in the ideational function of speech. They are, in other words, crucial stepping stones in a marvelously complex and uniquely human linkage of our thoughts to the intricate muscular system that allows man to articulate the meaningful sounds called words. When the speech cortex is delicately probed with tiny electrodes, the patient's reactions give us a crude inkling of what the thought-to-word linkage means to us.

Again the electrodes prevent speech, rather than produce it, but they do so in a far more fascinating way than in the case of the motor-control areas of vocalization. A patient, for example, may see and recognize a pencil while the electrode touches his brain, yet he is unable to say "pencil." He may talk about a stick with a sharp point with lead in the middle used for the purpose of writing on paper, but until the electrode is withdrawn he is unable to say "pencil." What's more, the electronically produced word blockage, though acting upon a cortical speech area, also restricts the patient's other communicative powers. Unable to speak a particular word, he similarly fails to comprehend it through reading and listening, and he cannot write the term.

Such a communication failure, as you may recognize, is symptomatic of a mild case of aphasia, a neurological disorder that often accompanies stroke. Aphasia results from brain damage that in a more drastic and lasting fashion produces what the scientists do in a gentle temporary way. The victim of the disorder, according to its severity, may lose any combination or all communication capabilities: reading, writing, speaking, listening or calculating—and in the worst cases the person is unable to relate meaning by gesture—beckoning "come here" with his hand, or nodding "yes" with his head—though the muscles needed for such movement work properly.

The parts of the cortex related to speech, especially the major area of the three, are keys to man's superiority over other animals. Here is the true gateway to the mind. On the far side lies one of the deepest mysteries of human existence for the gate encloses the storehouse of memory and the marvelous syntactical processes of thought, all of which remain a puzzle to us. But coming through the gate the evasive processes of thought are transformed into words that we use as freely as the air we breathe. If the gate is ever locked against its owner's will, as in the case of severe aphasia, the victim suffers one of the worst imaginable fates that a man can meet. If it happens in youth, the mind is locked against the world. If it happens with age the mind is locked against itself.

"The most precious and indispensable portion of the adult's cortex," explains Dr. Penfield, "is the major speech area. It might be worthwhile to forfeit other areas and so lose other functions in order to gain a cure [for some brain disorder], but never speech." The famous scientist and neurosurgeon thinks of our speech function as "the precious jewel of the brain."

THE PROTECTION OF SPEECH

The creator of man must also have considered the crucial nature of speech to humankind, for it is endowed with a degree of resilience enjoyed by only the highest order of cerebral functions. A brief look at nature's inclination to keep and protect our unique speech ability again reveals the primary role it plays in the communicative act so central to man's supremacy among all living things.

In roughly the first decade of life, human speech is protected by the brain's "plasticity." As stated above, the cortical speech areas in the normal brain are located on the organ's left hemisphere, but sometimes the neurosurgeon's electric probes discover them in the right hemisphere. The life history of these unusual cases is almost certain to reveal that at an early age, perhaps at birth or before, the person's brain was damaged on the left side. At the time of such an accident the organ exhibits a remarkable facility for moving the speech areas away from the damaged portion of the cortex to the other side of the brain. During the move the individual may lose his speech temporarily but then it returns to normal. This particular neurological insurance, however, runs out as the child moves up into his teens. The adult who sustains serious damage to the cortical areas of speech may well lose the capability. For instance, it may happen to the aphasia victim.

Yet in later years, cerebral plasticity seems to work to a degree in the more confined areas of the cortex within the left hemisphere. If part of a cortical speech area is damaged, the brain may cause nearby healthy tissue to take over in an attempt to restore the ability to speak. Stroke victims who suffer immediate loss of speech may have it returned, entirely or in part, because of this brain plasticity. Speech therapists can aid the process through special oral exercises which, in a sense, train the healthy parts of the brain that are attempting to replace the damaged tissues.

Another kind of cerebral insurance for speech, referred to as "redundancy," is evident in that the cortex has three speech areas rather than one. When scientists like Dr. Penfield apply their electric probes to these different areas one at a time, the patient may react the same way regardless of which area is being stimulated. This reveals, in other words, that many of the human speech functions are, in effect, in triplicate. Some of the three parts can therefore be lost without the loss of speech. One of the three speech areas, that in the uppermost part of the cortex, can be completely cut away with only a temporary disturbance to the patient's speech. This cannot be said for the other two areas, especially the one considered the major speech area.

Obviously the three territories are connected; however, it is interesting to note that the linkage is not along the comparatively exposed cortical surface, but underneath along protected routes. The dissection of human brains indicates that the speech areas are tied together through a part of the brain known as the "thalmus" which lies deep within the human head. If this well-protected center is damaged, perhaps by disease, the victim is likely to suffer severe speech problems.

COMPLEXITY REVEALED BY DAMAGE

While the creator of man recognized the overriding importance of speech capability, its protection was far from simple because the production and reception of speech is a vastly complicated neurological business. A slight notion of this complexity is gained if you consider some of the baffling problems incurred by different kinds of brain damage. Here are some examples:

A person may keep and use every word he ever learned, but by a certain neurological malfunction he may lose the ability to put the words together in grammatical form. Another cerebral failure can cause the victim to speak in a telegraphic style. Brain damage can wipe out one's ability to comprehend words and the letters that form them, but at the same time the individual experiences no trouble dealing with numbers. One kind of a brain lesion will prevent a person from speaking of inanimate objects, but he can talk of living things. The reverse is the case for another kind of damage. Or a victim may find himself unable to repeat words spoken to him, though he can personally use them with ease.

SUPERIOR SOUND EQUIPMENT

When this complex communication system controlled by the brain's speech areas is in good working condition, the owner is endowed with a mechanism unmatched in any other living being or man-made machine. Besides integrating thought and language on an intellectual level approached by no other creature, human speech works with unmatched sound-handling mechanisms.

First, man has been provided with bodily mechanisms which give him very fine control over the movement of air through his larynx. With it he can sustain a long, pure and simple sound. Few animals can do it and none as well as man. The gibbon's larynx is nearest that of humans, but the animal lacks the mental capacity to use it as we do. A beast whose mental powers approach ours, the chimpanzee, can seldom come up with the fine, sustained vocalization known to man for the animal's larynx is too complicated.

Second, man has been blessed with an epicritical ear that allows him to listen selectively to sounds and tell one from the other according to the source. The human listener, for example, can distinguish the calls of other creatures from the sounds of a footstep. This critical ability with sound is derived from man's highly developed cochlea of the internal ear, and from a unique distribution of nerve fibers through the brain.

Third, man has an unmatched ability to imitate what he hears. We often marvel at this capability in certain birds, but a normal human being can go far beyond any of his feathered friends when it comes to mocking other creatures.

Perhaps the most amazing fact about these three superior capabilities with sound is that they became simultaneously available to man along with the brain structure to use them in the language process.

Despite this complexity of speech, it has become one of man's least taxing, most natural acts, so much so that this in itself greatly determines how we look upon the spoken word. It has been a large factor in the neglect of oral language development as an important tool of learning and communication.

IV

The Neglected Differences

ONE DAY IN Washington, D. C., I telephoned the U.S. Office of Education and asked the information operator for someone who could discuss the teaching of speech. The inquiry entangled me in a sticky series of questions and answers.

"What do you mean?" asked the operator.

"Well, I mean *speech*," I replied.

"Speech? I don't understand."

"It's what you're doing. Speaking! Talking!"

"Yes, but . . ."

"Wait, let me start over. You have people there who specialize in reading?"

"Of course. Many."

"And writing?"

"Yes, I guess so."

"Now, how about speaking and listening? They certainly are important elements of human communication. You make your living with them."

The operator laughed and said, "Oh, dear, let me see. What might that come under?"

She eventually switched me to a man whose field is English teaching. He knew of the speech field, but seemed poorly informed of the role it played in the U.S. Office of Education.

THE STRANGE BUT NATURAL WORD

By nature, the spoken word suffers from problems of obscurity. It is constructed of fleeting sounds. Words that are spoken to us march by once and are gone. They are not arranged left to right in horizontal lines that can be seen, studied, revised, corrected, graded, parsed, copied, carried home, bound in a book or pinned to a bulletin board. Centuries of educators have been unable to put their hands on the spoken word as they have the written word. The latter has paraphernalia that can be touched and dealt with. As sculptors have preferred clay to mercury as their medium, teachers have chosen the written over the spoken word as theirs.

We use spoken communication so much with so little effort that it, like breathing, becomes an unnoticed part of existence. William Work, the Executive Secretary of the Speech Association of America, says: "Speaking is like walking. Children come to school doing it, so it seldom occurs to teachers that here is something to teach."

Until recent years it seldom occurred to educational researchers that spoken language was worth investigation. When Ralph G. Nichols of the University of Minnesota began his well-known study of listening, he found, according to the *Encyclopedia of Educational Research,* that by 1939 in the United States and England reading had been the subject of 1,951 published "scientific" studies, while its oral counterpart, listening, was discussed in only fourteen such published reports. We still have not fully investigated and put to work the full potential of the intricate and unique facility of speech reserved for man in the neurological structure of the human brain.

DIFFERENCES THAT MAKE THE DIFFERENCE

Comparisons of the spoken and written word reveal that they are alike chiefly because they employ the same words; otherwise, great differences form a deep gulf between these two primary channels of human communication. They are differences hardly ever considered in the education of our most educated people.

Over the centuries they have been noted, but in the language arts less and less has been done about them. Aristotle, for example, said: "It should be observed that each kind of rhetoric has its own appropriate style. The style of written prose is not that of spoken oratory... Both written and spoken have to be known." In more recent times some scientific studies have tried to pin down the differences between oral and written language. Let's consider two of the studies.

One was conducted by engineers of the Bell Telephone System around 1930 when some 1,800 telephone conversations on typical toll circuits terminating in New York City were audited. During one week an observer recorded only the nouns used in 500 conversations; a second week she noted only the verbs in another 500 conversations; the third week 500 conversations were audited for only adjectives and adverbs, and finally, in two sets of 150 conversations each, she recorded only prepositions and conjunctions, and then only pronouns and articles. The results of this tedious job were compared with a study of written matter made in a similar vein at Harvard University.

The second piece of research was conducted about a quarter of a century later at Queens College by an Associate Professor of Psychology, Milton W. Horowitz, who worked with a large number of people in a controlled experiment on speech and writing. Each subject was asked to pick a simple topic such as: "What does a good doctor mean to you?" After thinking about the topic for 30 seconds half the people were asked to write all they could about their selected subject, and half were asked to talk about theirs into a recording device. The psychologist then compared the two modes of communication.

Both studies provide considerable evidence to show that (1) while the spoken word has many advantages by being the most human, easy, natural form of communication, it (2) is low on the kind of discipline, precision and formality that might come from training.

FACILE AND FREE

The two pieces of research reached conclusions agreeing that spoken language is much more facile than written. It is more prolific with words, phrases and sentences, said Professor Horowitz. Written style, the telephone company investigators found, is self-conscious, and filled with qualifications and carefully chosen synonyms. They noted, however, that in spoken conversation, thought was the chief concern, while the speaker paid far less attention to his grammatical form of expression.

"The sentences are, indeed, likely to be shorter," said the report of the telephone company research. "They are often incomplete, in fact. But often in conversation even a single statement is completed only after a number of fumbling attempts, an oral manifestation of crystallizing thought, whereas in written matter the final expression alone would appear. In repetition of a thought, synonyms are less likely to be found in conversation than in written matter. Dependent clauses are less frequent than in written matter. Qualification and description often take the form of separate sentences, so that those words characteristic of involved construction tend to be less prominent in conversation, while the framework words, such as the auxiliary verbs and pronouns, are more intensively used."

The Queens College psychologist noted, as did the telephone company investigators, that the act of writing is done with an air of permanence. This seems to be a psychologically motivated feeling which tells us that what we write exists for the future while what we speak is only for now. Professor Horowitz's research showed that even the use of a tape or disc recording device for the speakers did not add a feeling of permanence which comes with raising a pen or using a typewriter.

Writing, he points out, is a more serious commitment than speech. This difference is recognized in the law where men are held more strictly to what they write than to what they say, for it is understood that in talking we are generally far less inhibited than in writing, and therefore are inclined to blurt out statements that are little more than slips of the tongue. Also oral expressions are more easily forgiven, with, "Oh, he just says that." But when we are formal and want commitment we demand, "Put that in writing!" In the written word, as both pieces of research found, we can expect more precision and relevant material, though the style is comparatively labored, duller, stodgier, more circumspect, more careful and more prosaic than the spoken word.

VOCABULARY DIFFERENCES

The telephone study had a lot to say about the oral and the written vocabularies—and indirectly about a failing of our schools in the teaching of vocabulary. From all the conversations, the observer tabulated a total of 80,000 words, but only 2,240 were different words. Moreover, the investigators found that of these different words only 121 constituted over half of the 80,000-word total. The pronouns "I" and "you" accounted for more than 7,500 words of the total. Compared with a similiar statistical breakdown in the Harvard study of written language, oral vocabulary was in dire poverty. The telephone company study, for example, showed that the 155 most used words in conversation represented 80 per cent of the total number used. Interpolation revealed that in the written study the same 80-per-cent level was represented by the 640 most used words. To put it another way, the writers were employing over four times the vocabulary found in telephone conversations. Such a comparison is a manifestation of how we neglect the spoken word in education, for it is hardly contestable that one's spoken vocabulary can be expanded through training. Also, the development of oral word usage, which naturally upgrades pronunciation, can automatically boost a person's written vocabulary, providing it is coordinated with efforts in spelling improvement.

THREE SPECIAL QUALITIES

Despite its weaknesses, which are often traceable to educational neglect, speech in its most human outgoing free form of language has qualities that are unique to itself and that hold numerous possibilities for the betterment of human discourse. First the spoken word, as a carrier of meaning, has a far greater capacity than the written word. Second, speech, of all our communicative skills, is the one most closely tied to our thought processes. And third, spoken words are more reflective of the human soul than other forms of expression. Let's consider each of these three qualities in detail.

1. THE CARRIER OF MEANING

That the spoken word has great capacity for meaning, has been expressed by Harry Shaw, author of the widely used textbook, *A Complete Course in Freshman English*. "When you talk," he says, "you do not depend upon words alone to tell your listener what you mean. Facial and bodily gestures can and do add much to the words themselves; you shrug a shoulder, wiggle a finger, raise an eyebrow, wink, clasp hands, bend forward or backward, grin or grimace, stamp your foot, nod or shake your head. The tone and stress of your voice can and do influence the meaning of words you speak: you yell or whisper; speak calmly or angrily; lower or raise your voice at the end of a statement or a question. Meaning in talk is affected by pauses and halts which are often as significant as the words themselves..."

"TONIGHT" WITH 50 MEANINGS. The amount of information, ideas and feelings that can be conveyed by a single spoken word is sometimes startling. Constantin Stanislavsky, co-founder of the Moscow Art Theater, is said to have asked each of his drama students to say the word "tonight" 50 times, flavoring it with that many different meanings, while classmates wrote down what they felt was conveyed by each interpretation. The word "tonight" shrieked by the voice of a man could carry enough meaning that it would require a page of writing to explain it all. The same shriek from a female voice might make it necessary to rewrite the entire page.

The meaning of spoken language is extremely susceptible to time, place and the people involved, because speech is a social act molded by thousands of ever-changing influences. The listeners at Gettysburg stood unaware of the fact that one of history's most memorable orations was being uttered as Abraham Lincoln made what were then described as "a few appropriate remarks." Patrick Henry's famous speech said nothing new to his listeners, but the time had truly come for the words that he spoke. As no one should dare say "fire" in a crowded theater, we learned on October 30, 1938, the dangers of broadcasting to a nation nervous from the exploits of Hitler that men from Mars had landed near Princeton, New Jersey.

In other words, spoken language is altered much more than its written counterpart by all that surrounds it. The spoken word is uttered in, and continually changed by, a vast and ever-changing stage setting. Dr. Jurgen Ruesch, a California research psychiatrist, says the language of gesture alone offers some 700,000 distinctly different signals while the largest English dictionaries define under 600,000 words.

For an idea of the speed and power with which nonverbal communication works, consider the results of an experiment conducted at Ohio State University by L. S. Harms. His subjects, 180 adults from different walks of life, were asked to listen, in carefully selected groups, to recordings of nine voices. The speakers had been chosen to represent three different occupational and educational levels determined by a special test designed to find a person's "status position" in society. Dr. Harms discovered that in only 10 to 15 seconds after a recording started, the typical listener, guided mainly by the sound of a voice, had formed a status judgment of the speaker and had thereby prejudged how credible the talker's material would be. The higher the status rating assigned by listeners to speakers, the higher the credibility rating.

From recent history we have some powerful examples of how spoken language is filled with unstated meaning. When non-German-speaking newspaper reporters heard Adolph Hitler's frenzied words, they often found themselves swept up by the power and persuasiveness of his voice and the setting he used it in. On the other side of the Atlantic the cultured, conviction-ladened voice of Franklin Roosevelt, speaking in friendly tones meant for the nation's living rooms, was feared by the President's opponents far more than anything he could write. One of the opposition, William Borah, by no means a novice to political address, refused to listen to FDR, but chose to read the text of Fireside Chats for fear that he might believe them if he heard them.

A most telling example of how the spoken word is forged by nonverbal influence was revealed by the first television debate of the 1960 election campaign. On radio it can be said that Richard Nixon won the first debate, but on television he lost. On the night of the debate Earl Mazo, a veteran political correspondent for the *New York Herald Tribune,* was at Hot Springs, Arkansas, covering the Southern Governor's Conference. The local television station carried the verbal encounter an hour after it happened, so people first heard the debate on network radio and then saw and heard it on television 60 minutes later. "The reaction of the governors and reporters with whom I first heard, then saw, the debate pointed up the difference between hearing and seeing," says Mazo in a discussion prepared for the Center for the Study of Democratic Institutions. "Before the encounter on radio was half finished every Kennedy partisan in the room was disparaging the whole idea of a fine upstanding young man like Senator Kennedy having to clash verbally with a crusty old professional debater like Vice-President Nixon. But the attitude changed immediately when the magic lantern of television came on.

"Careful reading of the texts would show that neither candidate really said much that night. Nor did either score any clearly distinctive points. Nixon was best on radio simply because his deep resonant voice conveyed more conviction, command and determination than Kennedy's higher-pitched voice and his Boston-Harvard accent. But on television, Kennedy looked sharper, more in control, more firm—his was the image of the man who could stand up to Khrushchev."

Analysis of the votes in the Nixon-Kennedy election revealed that the former Vice President did better where the debate had the largest radio audiences. Nine per cent of the audience in the West, where Nixon won, heard the debate by radio, while in the East, where he lost, only 2 per cent of the audience heard the debate by radio.

NATURAL TECHNIQUES FOR CLARITY. The cloak of unsaid meaning that richly clothes spoken language plays endless roles in our most routine personal communication. By the stress, pitch and pause found with everyone's speech we give oral language structure and clarity—and incidentally provide the basis for grammatical rules, especially punctuation, applied to written expression. But these attributes of speech go farther than any comparable ones in writing.

We are very much guided as to the rightness or wrongness of language, written and spoken, by how it sounds. When a written sentence seems to be wrong, for example, our first inclination is to say it out loud. From the time we start learning our mother tongue as infants, we aurally sense the word patterns of what we hear. They may be totally wrong, an example of the uneducated mind, but if we learn that these patterns are the comfortable ones in the speech around us, they become our way of talking—and writing. When we meet a different aural pattern of words, though correct in the eyes of the world's best grammarians, it can fray our auditory nerves. The acceptable patterns, of course, may change as we grow up or move from one stratum of society to another. The grammar that is poor according to the rules may sound fine to the ten-year-old but as he moves up the educational ladder, it is likely to irritate his new peers, and he too will soon find more aural comfort with the sounds of better grammar. Linguists and others believe that by putting this aural feeling for language to work, teachers can develop a most powerful tool for the general improvement of English in our schools.

AN ENDLESS SEARCH FOR UNDERSTANDING. With the nonverbal meaning of oral language we find a unique quality available to the spoken word that perhaps, as much as anything else, holds possibilities for the improvement of human understanding. When we converse, the words move back and forth among a great many unspoken signals that say whether or not understanding is being achieved. A vague look in a listener's eyes may reveal his lack of comprehension. An expression of boredom, a scowl, the flush of anger, the spark of a new thought, a smile, a smirk, a quizzical tilt of the head —and many other mannerisms serve as feedback from listeners. The signals often demand the restatements of ideas, which leads to a great deal of redundancy that is generally evident with spoken words.

Traditional grammarians studying oral expression (recorded in writing) have often seen such redundancy as proof that the spoken word vulgarizes language, but more likely it reveals a search for understanding. On the one hand the search is conducted by the talker who repeats and restates for the sake of clarifying his thoughts to the listener; on the other hand, his redundancy may mean he is clarifying his thoughts for himself, perhaps in order to improve their transmission (which is something we shall discuss below). While the resulting language may be turgid when transcribed, it can represent a high level of communication in the original oral discourse between particular people under particular circumstances.

Henry Nelson Wieman, the University of Chicago Professor Emeritus of Philosophy and Relgion, sums up these accoutrements of the spoken word when he talks about the "existential situation" of speech, which is described as "the actual, present set of conditions in which the speaker utters what he has to say." Professor Wieman talks of how they are used in what is called "creative interchange," or the kind of communication that does three things: "(1) creates an understanding in the listener for the viewpoint of the speaker; (2) integrates this viewpoint into the perspectives of the listener so that he has a more comprehensive understanding; (3) communicates the sense of good and evil so that each can be aware of the way the other values the alternative possibilities arising out of a situation."

Professor Wieman feels "this kind of interchange is a basic good in human life. It is the chief way in which error is corrected, knowledge expanded, values purged, insight deepened and appreciative understanding established among individuals, groups and peoples." He sees the development of such interchange in a democracy as "the high vocation and major responsibility of the teacher of speech." And he feels it "is the only way that democracy can be sustained and communicated to others."

2. CLOSENESS TO THOUGHT

Some authorities have said, in so many words, that thought and speech are nearly one and the same. The famous Johns Hopkins psychologist, the founder of the school of "behaviorism," John B. Watson, expressed the point of view that the human larynx was biologically connected with thinking, that the relationship was not only evident when we speak, but was also revealed in subvocal muscular responses. Dr. Watson felt that if this mechanical side didn't exist in what he considered to be the total thinking process, thought would not exist.

The psychologist's beliefs are cited in the report of the Queens College speech study wherein Professor Horowitz points out that today few authorities think of the mechanical side of language as part of thought. "Nevertheless," he adds, "it is very often largely a verbal process. Further verbal facility tied intimately to intelligence is the predominant mode of communication in the human being, and is probably the only major function that shows no deterioration in many of its manifestations with time."

CLEAR CIRCUIT TO THOUGHT. The psychologist notes how physiological design allows us to express our thinking much more easily by speaking than writing. "Writing . . . is labored and difficult," he says. "The fingers, wrist and arm are excellent instruments for prehension, for attack and defense, but writing does not fit them as speaking fits the larynx." From a biological point of view, speech has a less complicated, less artificial, more felicitous circuit, structure or relationship to the thought processes than has written expression.

This facility is evident in the very human trait of constantly putting thoughts into words. The Queens College researcher noted that the oral subjects of his experiment seemed to be driven to talk ceaselessly. Even a few seconds of silence appeared hard to bear and the talker was always pressed to continue. On the surface this oral obsession appeared to produce only aimless, irrelevant, repetitious and useless material, but a closer look revealed in nearly all the cases that the verbal rambling generated many new ideas. A comparison of the written and spoken material composed by the experiment's subjects revealed that despite its verbosity, the spoken effort per unit of time produced more ideas and elaboration of ideas than the written material, although this was not the case when the number of ideas per word per unit of time was considered.

The verbal rambling that goes with the process of locating ourselves and our ideas in the world of thought is most evident in young children who are forever orally mulling things over—just talking in what often seems like a meaningless line of repetitious chatter, or through a perplexing, endless series of questions. One researcher decided to record his children's questions for a single day. His three-year-old child was tucked into bed and finally fell asleep after 376 questions. His four-year-old was finally stopped by the sand man on the 397th. In another study everything that was stated by a two-year-old girl was recorded from 7:00 A.M. to 7:30 P.M. Here is but a drop of her rivers of oral activity, recorded as she sat with her grandmother:

"I'm sewing a button—I found a big button, too. That's the best one. Now it'll be all right. On this side. Now I make a nightgown. Is that a knot? Helen don't have a very large buttonhole either. Cut it now. Now the button is sewed on. Now I have to get another string. Here's a pad—didy to go underneath. Here's the woolen blanket. I found it. Helen has some more sewing to do. Helen wants to set a buttonhole on it. What kind of buttonhole? What kind of buttonhole? That's too little. That's not very large. I'm not ready."

THE DIFFERENCE IN AUDIENCES. As a person writes, you may say in summary, he works chiefly for his audience, while the talker to a large extent may speak with himself. In his unending, psychologically driven talk, filled with what often seems like the verbal excess that in writing receives the editorial knife, the talker exercises his own mental processes. The listening audience is not only an object of communication, but is an excuse for turning over and testing one's thoughts. "Having more 'facility,' speaking can create an 'active' channel which drains energy from other channels," says Professor Horowitz. "Such uses of energy frequently produce novel thoughts. To me, this is an exciting finding."

3. THE REFLECTION OF THE SOUL

Through the gregarious, outgoing form of the spoken word, we release our true feelings far more easily than in the solitary, cautious act of taking a pen in hand. Indeed, it is only a great novelist who touches in writing the inner feelings that most of us express with little conscious effort in everyday speech. It is interesting that many of the most memorable novels were written under great pressure, usually financial, forcing the writer to work fast and with abandon, thereby increasing the chances of his saying what he thought —as seems to happen with the easy flow of speech. But the great majority of writers cannot help but hide their true feelings in the cautious stiffness of the written word.

Thomas Burke has said that ". . . any man who is in danger of attention from posterity, and wishes to hide certain things, will find no better hiding place than under the arclights of autobiography." And Edgar Allan Poe once concluded that any man "seeking immortal renown" could "revolutionize, at one effort, the universal world of thought, human opinion and human sentiment," if he could only "write and publish a very little book. Its title should be simple—a few plain words—*My Heart Laid Bare*. But this little book must be true to its title."

A PROBE OF PSYCHIC LAYERS. While many different methods and theories of psychotherapy exist, their exponents commonly recognize that through a patient's speech a skilled therapist has the greatest opportunity to tap a human being's deepest psychic layers. With the natural ease of speech, a person is more likely to give freely of his inner truths than he would through the labored formality of writing with its attendant feelings of permanence that naturally inhibit an individual. But more important to the therapist is the self-communicative possibilities of the spoken word, briefly touched on above. The therapist, who has to be an especially skillful listener, provides his patient with the chance to establish communication between his own various psychic layers. You might say the patient is allowed to develop a conversation between his conscious stream of thinking and those deeply repressed thoughts so difficult to reach and deal with.

This kind of inner-directed conversation is not limited to a therapist's office. Day by day much of everyone's endless, often meaningless talk, is a reflection of the never-completed human effort to unlock the secrets of self. If people could generally become aware of this universal trait, and treat it with understanding, the results would benefit all human communication.

And everything that is said here about speech reaching the core of individuals can also be applied to whole societies. Speech in its colloquial form is a mirror of the society it binds together. Literature, of course, tells a great deal about the people it attempts to portray, but it reveals only a fraction of what is reflected by the native tongue.

In summary we can say that the spoken and written words, with their vast and varied differences can hardly be treated as one and the same discipline. The differences strike at the core of the assumption held by so many teachers, that if they teach the first two Rs their pupils will automatically speak and listen well. The differences re-emphasize our central question here: Why do we so badly neglect the science and art of spoken language in education?

V

Teaching
the Mother Tongue

THE TEACHING OF English uses up more time and personnel than any other subject in all of our schools below the graduate and professional level. A progress report of The Panel on Educational Research and Development (under the President's Science Advisory Committee) pointed out that "more than 90,000 secondary-school teachers and more than 11,000 college and university teachers are engaged primarily in teaching English, while almost all of the nearly 900,000 elementary-school teachers devote a substantial portion of their time to this task." The teaching of our native tongue, points out the panel, appears under many "guises" ranging from learning to read to linguistics and semantics. "But despite this enormous investment in instruction in English," says the report, "many students when they leave school do not read well enough or write well enough to meet the practical demands of our times." (And I am sure the author of the report would have gladly added "speak" and "listen" to this sentence had he been prompted to do so.)

"What's wrong with English?" is a question much discussed in educational circles. The National Council of Teachers of English has become most analytical and highly critical of its own work. The U.S. Office of Education established

"Project English" (renamed, "U.S.O.E. English Program") through which it is supporting considerable research aimed at the improvement of English teaching from kindergarten through college and graduate school. New English textbooks reflect the search for new ways to teach our own language. And the subject is well aired in educational journals, as well as more popular publications.

GRUESOME GRAMMAR

In this discussion one of the most heated areas centers around the traditional part of English teaching that many an adult will readily agree was what made the study of his mother tongue an unhappy, unprofitable experience. It is called "grammar."

In his school days, the typical adult recalls, there was reading which put him in touch with literature, but for the second R, writing, the English teacher shifted a pedagogical gear and taught grammar. Here one was administered the rules for grammatically acceptable writing, though he seldom learned how to formulate his thoughts with clarity in writing. The same rules were also applied to speech by an occasional prompt from a teacher—which pretty much constituted the full course of study on how to talk with clarity. In other words, from dull, perplexing rules, mainly concerned with the acceptable arrangement of words, a person was expected to learn the difficult skill or art of transferring ideas from one human to another chiefly through writing.

The assumption seemed to be that you came to school able to communicate—obviously through talking, from which one discovered how to write merely by learning to copy his own talk. The rules of grammar would simply insure that one translated what he copied in a fashion acceptable to the educated mind prevalent in the century when the rules were formulated and fixed. It might be compared with expecting a

nonflier to learn how to pilot a jet airliner by studying the
air traffic regulations of an earlier aviation era.

GRAMMAR INSTEAD OF LANGUAGE

The grammatical-rules-first approach to language is still
with us and much lamented by the critics of English teaching. In a special issue of the Harvard *Educational Review* on
"Language and Learning," H. A. Gleason, Jr., of the Hart-
ford Seminary Foundation, deplores the fact that "adult
Americans are badly informed about language," that "they
have no better insight into their own English tongue than
into language in general." He continues: "This lack of insight is the more disturbing when it is remembered that our
schools devote a larger part of the educational effort to 'language arts' and to 'English' than to any other subject matter.
It might appear that the shortcomings cannot have arisen
simply from lack of attention. But on closer examination, we
find that language itself actually receives little direct consideration in most segments of this sadly riven curriculum and is
totally neglected in others. The result of this prevailing neglect is an anomaly: Within what is often called the 'language
curriculum' the study of language is segregated as 'grammar.' "

GRAMMAR IS TO WRITE

Historically, grammar is devoted to sight and not sound.
Look up the word in Webster's, along with the word "graphic"; and you find the two stem from the same Greek word
graphein, to write. The history of grammar reveals that it is
devoted so much to the written word that it sometimes seems
to deny that a spoken language exists.

An analysis by Walter J. Ong, S.J., Associate Professor of
English at St. Louis University, of a well-known eighteenth-

century English grammarian, James Harris, reveals the denial of sound that grew up with traditional grammar and is still remarkably well preserved in much of this century's grammar instruction. Father Ong noted that Harris's writing said "in effect, that oral speech is the effect of reading, reading the effect of writing, and writing the effect of grammar. Or in reverse, the principles of grammar 'cause' writing, writing 'causes' reading, and reading 'causes' oral speech."

Father Ong's comment on such reasoning is stated thusly: "This altogether shipshape account blinks entirely the simple fact that so far are reading and writing from 'causing' speech that most men who have lived in the world have done all their [formal communicating through] speaking and the evolution of language has pursued nearly its entire course without reading or writing at all."

The blind tendency of early language scientists and teachers to work solely with the "graphic," written word is traced by many authorities to the inability to grapple with sound. "Studying written speech," says Father Ong, "is, of course, far simpler than studying spoken speech, and it is not strange that the early attempts to scientize speech, almost without exception until just a few years ago, veer toward the consideration of written or literary language exclusively, disregarding or slurring over the fact that this is language at second remove . . . sound is taken not as existing in its own right but as a derivative of letters. It exists as second remove."

JESPERSEN'S QUESTIONS

A break in this kind of thinking appeared in the early twentieth century when the founding fathers of modern linguistics were presenting their theories of language. The most famous, the Danish philologist Otto Jespersen, saw language not as the outgrowth of static formulas set forth by rules of grammar that theoretically could cover all the structural word patterns, but as a "human activity—activity on the part of one individual to make himself understood by another, and activity on the part of that other to understand what was in the mind of the first." Jespersen sensed and stated that the scientists of language before him had become too involved with the written word. He said that in this preoccupation, words were treated as objects which lived, not as part of human activity, but in their own right. The Dane in 1924, in his renowned volume, *The Philosophy of Grammar*, presented his readers with a contradiction to the traditional notions which held the written word supreme. "The spoken and the heard word," said Jespersen, "is the primary form of language."

Today the theories set forth by Jespersen and his fellow linguistic scientists are on the move, and many of those who search for more effective English teaching see the need for focusing on language as a human activity rather than a graphic object described by the rules of grammar. In this change of focus the emphasis moves ever so slowly from the written to the spoken word.

"Grammar teaching has always been narrowly focused on one form of standard English, the infinite variety of speech and writing habits receiving only silent neglect," says H. A. Gleason in his piece in the 1964 special language issue of the *Harvard Educational Review*. "Such a partial picture is so unreal as to have cast doubt in the minds of many on the whole structure of grammar. [A]... need, then, is to broaden the concern of grammar teaching to comprehend more than a single form of the language. Something of this sort is already under way and, increasingly, this segment of the whole is being referred to as 'language' rather than as 'grammar.' What is being done is generally good, but often far too limited."

SAME GRAMMAR, NEW FROSTING

The slow pace is better understood when we realize how far behind Jespersen's ideas of half a century ago are the ideas and methods of those who teach English every day in most of our schools. Today's grammar, now frosted with new titles, more often than not is the same recipe for what tasted so badly when today's adult was learning his mother tongue. A modern linguist, Andrew Schiller, Associate Professor of English at the University of Illinois, says that "we are automatically convinced that today's fashions [in English teaching] represent progress. Yet, though my children find my old fountain pen as quaint as a quill, they are still being taught the grammar Thomas Jefferson learned."

But if a teacher stuck in the old grammarial rut does want to drop it in favor of a new more enlightened approach, he has difficulty finding a towing service. While the educational journals and other literature have a good inventory of theory and discussion, they are notably bare of plain, understandable how-to-do-it material. It is fine to talk about the failings of the English teacher, but until we provide her with the day-to-day know-how of effective language instruction, our schools are likely to continue with the rules that Thomas Jefferson learned. Ruth I. Golden of the Detroit public schools says it in a most straightforward way: "We cannot apply the old rules, and yet there are no new ones to take their place."

SPOKEN FOREIGN TONGUES

English teachers, it seems, might profit from what has happened in foreign-language instruction and in the teaching of English as a second language. The emphasis over the past sev-

eral years has, through the "direct method," shifted from a
written to a spoken approach. The written has by no means
been dropped, but the student's groundwork for learning a
new language is laid through the spoken form. The study of
grammar, once considered a primary first step for acquisition
of a foreign tongue, is now detained to a point in time when
the student is already speaking his new language Then
grammar is offered much more sensibly as a set of rules which
formulate what the pupil already knows and uses. Grammar,
as a first step, has been replaced by an oral learning of patterns
on which the language is built. They are learned by oral repetition, through the give and take of questions and answers
spoken in the new language only, and by other spoken
means.

With the oral approach, whose success is well established,
a question often arises: The student learns to speak, but does
he learn to read? While the answer is "yes," the question itself reflects a basic misunderstanding that harks back to the
old notion that in the learning of language the rules of writing should come first. Such thinking did not look upon language as a basic raw material to be mentally assimilated and
then used in all modes of communication: reading, writing,
speaking and listening.

In the direct method, where one might say the horse has
been returned to the front of the cart, oral procedures have
been found to be the most advantageous for learning a language, not solely to speak it, but for acquiring the language
itself. The method seems to hold the best possibilities for circumventing the laborious process of translating word-by-
word by leading the student directly into a way of thinking
and speaking in the language itself, as we do with our mother
tongue. Then, with the new language itself in mind, as opposed to resorting continually to a mental translating system,
reading naturally comes more easily than in the old method.
In other words, the student, in his new reading experience,

finds himself dealing directly in raw material with which he is well familiarized.

THE BRAIN AND LANGUAGE LEARNING

The learning of additional languages has intensely interested the Montreal scientist and neurosurgeon, Wilder Penfield, who with his colleagues has been so instrumental in mapping the brain's speech functions. What he has found may also have meaning for the teaching of the mother tongue. Dr. Penfield has some fascinating neurological evidence indicating that the human facility for learning language goes through a major physiological change at the end of life's first decade, or thereabouts. Before this age parts of the brain related to the speech cortex are involved in developing neurological switch mechanisms that have a great deal to do with how we can accept new languages. As the child passes the age of 10 or 12 this basic work of the brain comes to an end, and in a sense the organ is ready to go to work with the language or languages it has acquired. But in the first decade, Dr. Penfield has found, the brain is at its optimum for developing switch mechanisms that allow the individual to shift his speech and mental processes from one language to another "without confusion, without translation, without a mother-tongue accent."

Such a finding, of course, would indicate a need to expose the very young to the extra languages he is expected to acquire. When exposed through a direct, oral contact for enough time the youngster, according to Dr. Penfield's theories, has the opportunity to develop the cerebral switch equipment that allows him to work directly in the new language, without confusion, translation or an accent. After the first decade, however, brain changes mean that new tongues now must come by way of translation.

However, the individual exposed to more than one

tongue in early life seems also to have developed neurological advantages for language learning in later life. "A unilingual adult," says Dr. Penfield, "who begins the learning of a second language late speaks it with a mother-tongue accent and tends to learn by translation. However, the adult who has previously learned some other second language in childhood is likely to learn a later third and fourth language faster and better than a unilingual adult. This greater facility of the bilingual adult may be due to the well-developed switch mechanism which he acquired in childhood. He is able to switch off the mother tongue easily, and thus to learn directly."

TRAINING THE BRAIN

Such evidence leads one to speculate if speech, more than our other communicative skills, has not the making of powerful tools for what Dr. Penfield calls "training of the brain," a process that goes beyond solely the learning of language. In this vein indications are cropping up that the quality of oral exercise experienced in the earliest years of life may have a direct bearing on development of intelligence.

For example, a study of ten-year-olds supported by the Carnegie Foundation at McGill University revealed that bilingual youngsters showed a greater level of intelligence than comparable children who knew but one language. In another instance, a University of California psychologist, Arthur Jensen, whose research delves into how children learn, has reported: "It has been found that reading aloud to children for a short time every day from the ages of one to two, even before any real 'understanding' is possible, not only is highly enjoyable to them but has significant later effects on speech and language development, reading ability and the I.Q."

A most notable discussion of this matter is found in the work of Benjamin S. Bloom, Professor of Education at the

University of Chicago, whose book, *Stability and Change in Human Characteristics,* assesses the effects of environment on intelligence. In this volume, based on "many longitudinal studies reported in this country and abroad during the last fifty years," Professor Bloom says: "...a conservative estimate of the effect of extreme environments on intelligence is about twenty I.Q. points This could mean the difference between a life in an institution for the feebleminded or a productive life in society. It could mean the difference between a professional career and an occupation which is at the semi-skilled or unskilled level."

The verbal environment to which children are exposed appears to be a leading factor in the development of intelligence. The Chicago educator states: "Since verbal ability represents a very important part of most general intelligence tests, it is likely that environments which include good models of the language will stimulate the development of language which will stimulate the development of general intelligence, whereas environments in which the models of language usage are poor and which discourage language development retard or block the development of general intelligence." Consider the import of such a statement in view of what we know about spoken language being by far the most used form of language.

POSSIBLE NEW TOOLS

In the neglected spoken word may be the raw material for educational tools that can finally lead the way to the success in the teaching of our own tongue that now seems to evade us so often with present methods devoted to the written word. This, however, is not likely until our efforts are directed at the whole of human communication.

The type of inclusive effort that is needed may develop in the newly established Human Communication Program in the National Institute of Health as one of eight scientific programs in the division called the National Institute of Child Health and Human Development. The program, with Norman F. Gerrie as its director, has this stated purpose: "Support of research activities and research training to investigate the role of the communicative process in, and its impact upon, human growth and development. Human communication is viewed as the vital process comprising the complex and interrelated biological, behavioral and social phenomena whereby information is transferred between the human being and his physical and social environment."

Here are some of the problems that Dr. Gerrie is concerned with:

"How does the child make the transition from the birth cry to comprehensible language?"

"What are the predisposing biological and psychological factors essential to the acquisition of reading skills?"

"How does the human being learn to convert speech-sound information into units of discourse?"

"How much strain can be placed on memory span before the message is lost?"

"To identify appropriate nonredundant cues in the speech signal which transmit information."

And finally what Institute researchers label a "major problem":

"To relate the development and function of the communicative process to the development of the individual."

VI

From Rhetoric
to the Shades
of Elocution

IN 1771 a wealthy Boston merchant, Nicholas Boylston, died leaving a will which stated: "I give & bequeath unto the President & Fellows of Harvard College in Cambridge in the County of Middlesex the sum of one thousand five hundred Pounds lawful money... toward the Support and Maintenance of some well Qualified Person who shall be elected by the President and Fellows of said College for the time being and approved of by the Overseers of said College to be the Professor of Rhetoric and Oratory...." The money remained unused by Harvard for over thirty years until Boylston's heirs threatened a suit to recover the funds. The threat prompted action in Cambridge, the Boylston Professorship of Rhetoric and Oratory was established, and on June 24, 1805, John Quincy Adams, who was to become the sixth President of the United States, was elected as the first Boylston Professor. This chair of Rhetoric and Oratory still exists at Harvard University, though at this writing it has been temporarily vacant since the retirement in 1962 of Archibald MacLeish.

The changing purpose of the Boylston Professorship in the 157 years from Adams to MacLeish is illustrative of what has generally happened to spoken-language education in America.

John Quincy Adams gave his first lecture in the new Harvard chair on July 11, 1806, and in his diary he wrote that his new course in rhetoric and oratory was "an undertaking of magnitude and importance." For the next three years the future President appeared at Harvard every Friday to meet with his students. In the mornings beginning at 10 o'clock he taught rhetoric and in the afternoons commencing at two he served as a listener and critic of student declamations. In his new position Adams concerned himself strictly with rhetoric in the traditional sense of studying the development and use of oral language.

Relying heavily on the teachings of Aristotle, Cicero and Quintilian, he followed four study areas which the Harvard Overseers had asked that he cover. First was "invention," which dealt with the problems of selecting and preparing material for spoken address. Next was "disposition," which had to do with the organization of oral material. Third was "style" of oral composition. And finally, "pronunciation" covered the actual delivery by voice and gesture. Adams, deeply devoted to the purposes and responsibilities of human speech, held that it was a "necessary adjunct and vehicle of reason" which man could put to good use in "rational intercourse with his fellow creatures and of humble communion with his God."

Adams' professorship was succeeded for the large part of a decade by Joseph McKean who also followed the precepts of the ancients in teaching rhetoric and oratory. Then came the man who was probably the most famous of all Boylston Professors, Edward T. Channing, his tenure running from 1819 to 1851. In this period a shift of emphasis from the spoken to the written word was evident, though Channing was still deeply concerned with the good use of oral language. The need was great, for Harvard graduates were usually destined for one of two professions, the law or the ministry, where good speech was mandatory.

The third Boylston Professor stressed that *what* one said took precedence over how it was said. He wrote that rhetoric should be concerned with "all communication by language and designed to make it efficient." Rhetoric, he said, "does not ask whether a man is to be a speaker or writer,—a poet, philosopher or debater; but simply,—is it his wish to be put in the right way of communicating his mind with power to others, by spoken or written."

Regardless of whether a student sought to be a writer or speaker, Channing's training was the same. But the great teacher did not neglect the differences between the two forms of communication. His lectures painstakingly pointed out that to be successful the nature of speaking had to be linked carefully with the nature of the audience. He stressed that, "The orator is the creature of the circumstances in which he is placed." Said Channing: "To have sway, the orator must be something more than what we call a man of ability. He must have a talent for his place." He emphasized that this talent should not be misused by emotionally persuading listeners while circumventing their powers of judgment. Out of such teachings came some of America's greatest writers and orators, men who dominated the field of letters for the remainder of the nineteenth century.

In *The Flowering of New England*, Van Wyck Brooks talked about Dr. Channing. "Their [the Harvard students'] scholarship was sure to be exacting," said Brooks, "especially when Edward Tyrrel Channing . . . became Professor of Rhetoric,—two years after the birth of a Concord boy, Henry Thoreau by name, who was to acknowledge, in later years, that he had learned to write as Channing's pupil. In fact, the whole New England 'renaissance' was to spring so largely from Channing's pupils, Emerson, Holmes, Dana, Motley, Parkman, to name only a few, that the question might have been asked, Did Channing cause it?"

The great names from Channing's classes not only became the century's most noted writers, but in their day, as in the case of Emerson, were listed among the great orators. One was James Russell Lowell who, as the American minister to Great Britain, became one of England's most sought after lecturers. "The English, not prone to concede pre-eminence in anything to anyone not English," said one writer about Lowell, "confessed his superiority in this difficult art."

After Edward T. Channing the Harvard chair of rhetoric and oratory quickly changed from the spoken almost entirely to the written word in keeping with developments at Harvard and in the nation. The students, no longer confined largely to law and the ministry, were entering medicine, engineering, the sciences and business. Improvements in printing in America were flooding people with the printed word. And the Harvard classes were growing too large for easy, individual attention so important to oral work. By the end of the nineteenth century Harvard students were being warned that unless they could exhibit great writing skill they were lost at Cambridge.

Channing's successor at mid-century was Francis J. Child who, according to Samuel Eliot Morison's volume, *The Development of Harvard University*, "first saw the possibilities of English as a factor in general scholarship." By the time he left the chair of rhetoric and oratory, Child had shifted its focus to the study of English and he had become "Professor of English." The next Boylston Professor, Adams Sherman Hill, who held the chair from 1876 to 1904 wrote a widely used text, *The Principles of Rhetoric*, in which the spoken word was all but forsaken by the Boylston Professor, for the book's material was directed chiefly to the writer, and oratory was not discussed at all.

During this period the student interested in speech improvement was likely to be directed to the teachers of elocution who were then enjoying great popularity. In direct contrast to the classical rhetoricians, elocutionists were infatuated with *how* an individual spoke and much less concerned with what he said.

This century's five Boylston Professors have not dealt formally with oratory, but have focused upon the composition of prose and poetry, and the study of literature. However, one of the five certainly knew and practiced the powers of spoken language. He was Charles Townsend Copeland, known to his students as "Copey," the personality who is said to have influenced Franklin Delano Roosevelt's speaking more than anyone else at Harvard.

Today speech receives but token attention at Harvard University. It does not have a speech department, though courses in "Speech Improvement, Public Speaking, Persuasion, and Argument" are taught by two members of the English Department, Professor Frederick C. Packard, Jr., and Associate Professor Harry P. Kerr. Their work includes the coaching of a debate team and one of the professors coaches Harvard Divinity School students.

WHEN READING WAS SPEAKING

As true with the Boylston Professorship, the spoken word since 1800 has been severed from its written counterpart in education in general. In the early nineteenth century a leading course of study was labeled "reading," but the similarity with today's reading ends pretty much with the name, for chiefly it meant learning to read aloud. Instructions establishing these early schools revealed their concern with teaching people to pronounce, articulate, project and, sometimes, to give oral expression to the written word.

In Boston in 1821, for instance, requirements for primary

grades read like this: "The fourth or youngest class shall
stand up with due ceremony at as great a distance from the
instructor as possible, and read with a distinct and audible
tone of voice in words of one syllable. No one of this class
shall be advanced to the third or higher class who cannot read
deliberately and correctly in words of one or two syllables."

This oral reading was a most mechanical treatment of
speech. Students were continually told to raise their voices, to
"speak up loud," and to read the words clearly. Another frequent admonition was to "mind the stops and marks," which
reflected attention to punctuation in oral reading. In some
instances youngsters were taught to measure their stops. A
comma, for example, called for a pause measured by a count
of one and a semicolon prompted a pause for a count of two.

Meanwhile, little attention was paid to the oral interpretation of meaning from the written word. This came later in
the century, but its absence in the earliest schools indicates to
some that the teaching was poor. Little training or educational insight is needed to tell students to speak up, to speak
clearly or mind the stops and marks, but it takes considerable
understanding to convey how one can read and truly bring
the words alive.

SPEECH FOR THE NEW DEMOCRACY

Early nineteenth-century students who continued into
the secondary schools still met with stiff oral-reading requirements, but in addition they received practice in the direct use
of the spoken word. These schools, especially the academies,
reflected the classical tradition passed down from schools of
higher learning such as Harvard. Andover, for example, required its teachers to consider the same elements of rhetoric
that John Quincy Adams was teaching as Harvard's Boylston
Professor. In New Hampshire, Exeter's teachers were charged
to develop oratory, declamation and "exercises of a forensic

kind." The tenets of America's new democracy were becoming better understood and the idea that all men were to play a part in government was more clearly realized. This in turn prompted educators, especially in the secondary schools, to recognize the need for educating all men. The ability to speak well in order to play one's role in the new government was considered a necessity.

Recognition that good speech was the mark of an educated man was not limited to the teachers in early America, but was something that education-interested parents seemed to sense. This undoubtedly was reflected in all the extracurricular speech activities: debates, dialogues, declamations, plays and other oral activities popular in nineteenth-century education. They were often as much a community function as today's sporting events. Many schools and towns formed debating societies, and prizes and awards for oral excellence were offered students.

In his memoirs, Cordell Hull tells of how important such activities were in the secondary schools of the 1880s: "The parents of the Willow Grove section were generally farmers with very limited education, but they were deadly in earnest that their children should get the utmost from their schooling. It was they who established a debating society at the schoolhouse so that their children could develop themselves in debate. They attended the debates and followed the arguments closely and seriously. They would not stand for levity. I remember that at one of the debates various parents rose and protested that some of us had not fully prepared our arguments."

Little wonder that nineteenth-century parents considered the articulate man a successful, educated man, for the skilled orator was a highly respected individual in expanding America. The public competition for the citizens' attention, through advertising and the like, was not nearly as great as it would be later, so lecturers were an unmatched source of fresh thoughts and information for the people who eventually would be supplied by the outpouring of newspapers, books, magazines and then, much later, by radio and television.

Few of us realize what a momentous event it was when a well-known orator appeared. This fact is impressed on anyone who may visit a picnic area in a small forest opening on a lonely mountain in southern Vermont. At one side picnickers see a metal marker on a large stone explaining that this site once was the scene of a lecture by Daniel Webster, well before the Civil War. Most startling is the notation that thousands of people drove there by horse and wagon from all over that part of New England to hear the great orator.

Orators like Webster met a need in America where the people sought leaders who could speak up above the boisterous frontiersmen. The historian, Henry Steele Commager, characterized the oration-loving American thusly:

"He was sentimental about Nature in her grander aspects and liked rolling rhetoric in his orators. He thought the whole history of his country romantic and heroic and on every Fourth of July and Decoration Day indulged in orgies of sentiment."

HOLBROOK'S LYCEUM

The popularity of lectures in America was borne out in the rapid growth of an institution started at Millbury, Massachusetts, by Josiah Holbrook. In 1826 he established a village Lyceum with a few farmers and mechanics who came to hear Holbrook's lectures on science. The idea was appropriate to its time and soon Massachusetts had nearly a hundred Lyceums which were formally organized at a Boston convention attended by Daniel Webster and Edward Everett, the orator who spoke with Lincoln at Gettysburg. The Lyceum became a unique adult-education movement in America and it flourished up to the Civil War. Town after town offered culture through the Lyceum. Many included museums with mineral exhibits, natural-history collections and libraries, but always central to the Lyceum was a hall and platform for visiting lecturers. The oratory was supplied by many names, including some of the best known of the century. Their topics were varied and often rich; the Lyceum orators spoke of travel, literature, science, fine arts, philosophy, religion, politics and other subjects.

One of the American Lyceum's most famous speakers was Ralph Waldo Emerson, who had always loved oratory and found the new movement made to his order. Moreover he discovered in the Lyceum an opportunity to speak to all kinds of Americans in a new free form of prose. Van Wyck Brooks says in his biography of Emerson that "here was a pulpit that made other pulpits tame and ineffectual. No need for a cold mechanical preparation, a decorous delivery, no stiff conventions that prescribed a method. Everything was admissible, philosophy, ethics, divinity, criticism, poetry, all the breadth and variety of conversation. What an opportunity for painting in fire his thought—for being agitated, to agitate! Here he could lay himself out prodigally on the subject of the hour, here he might hope for nectar and enchantment."

Emerson found the Lyceum, says Brooks, "a stringent test for the wares of a man of letters. Could he hold stout farmers upright on their benches or stop the gossip around the door by a mere discussion of art or manners? Not always by any means. At times the audience was cold and unresponsive and his best efforts were drowned as it were in ice-water. But usually he found the experience exhilarating."

The biographer also gives us an interesting picture of the Lyceum visited by Emerson: "Pleasant...were those evenings in country meeting-houses when the snow sparkled under the moon and the whole neighbourhood came stamping in, smothered in shawl and muffler, when the sleigh-bells tinkled up to the door and the dim oil lamps flared under the low ceiling, and the boys and girls gathered round the stove giggling and munching apples."

ELOCUTION: DEVOTION TO VOICE

One year after Josiah Holbrook formed the first Lyceum, a new book marked the beginning of another American speech movement, also a response to the new nation's loud and vociferous character. *The Philosophy of the Human Voice* came from the pen of Dr. James Rush, son of Dr. Benjamin Rush, signer of the Declaration of Independence. James, like his father, was interested in the intellectual functioning of the mind, and he contended that thought and speech were the same. "To describe the mind," he once wrote, ". . . it is necessary to show the inseparable connection between thought and voice; with their influences on each other: for they cannot, separately, be known." Such thinking, bolstered by his medical background, led Dr. Rush to consider the production of sound as related to the vocalization of thought, and to write his famous book which for its day was an excellent treatise on speech physiology. He believed that the volume could make a significant contribution to rhetoricians by providing an understanding of speech mechanics. The work did serve as such and is still thought of as an important contribution to the foundations of speech therapy and other physiological-psychological areas of speech production.

But Dr. Rush's work played a role that he probably never intended for it. It became a basic book for a field of speech education, already grown up in England, that was catching the interest of Americans. Known as the "elocutionary movement," it had benefits to offer the spoken word, but the movement's overenthusiastic followers did damage that to this day psychologically affects the thinking of educators, especially in the English-teaching profession.

Dr. Rush's book was widely read when orators were so popular in nineteenth-century America and thousands of people wanted gold-plated voices. As so often happens with a popular desire for speech improvement, the mechanics of voice became the center of attention while the content, idea-development side of the spoken word was neglected. Dr. Rush's book seemed to offer the kind of raw material that the voice-conscious public wanted, and the new breed of American elocutionist carried it on from there.

ACCEPTANCE, THEN DISGRACE

In the last seventy years of the 1800s elocution was widely accepted, even at our most honored educational institutions, but by the end of the period it fell in disgrace. The American elocutionists were a vigorous group of teachers who were engrossed in the correct mechanical production of human speech. While this intense interest laid the groundwork for a lot of today's widely accepted speech-correction work, the elocutionists chiefly focused on the care and discipline of the human voice so that it might be finely controlled as an accomplished violinist would play his instrument. Many elocutionists dealt with the human process of vocalization in such detail that it is now hard to believe.

For instance, Jonathan Barber, a Harvard teacher wrote a book, *Grammar of Elocution* in which he gives an ultra-detailed description of how to pronounce the word "man" properly. "In pronouncing the word *man*," he states, "the lips are first intentionally brought together and pressed in a certain way against each other, and air being at the same time forcibly impelled from the throat, a sound is heard which somewhat resembles the lowing of an ox." The paragraph continues for nearly 400 words minutely dissecting the sound of the three-letter word, and concludes: "After the three sounds of the word have thus been separately pronounced, let *man* be slowly uttered, so that each separate sound and the coalescence of them with each other, may be distinctly perceived at the same time."

With the American desire to speak well, elocutionary teaching was much in demand. Many elocution books followed the one by Dr. Rush. When colleges like Harvard and Yale offered the voice training to their students it raised the subject's stature. One of the best-known elocutionists was Reverend Ebenezer Porter, the Bartlett Professor of Sacred Rhetoric at Andover Seminary. A large number of private elocution schools were opened around the nation, like the Vocal and Polyglot Gymnasium run by Andrew Comstock in Philadelphia, the Emerson School of Oratory in Boston, and the Columbia School of Expression in Chicago. Americans were also taught elocution by itinerant instructors of the new and popular art. Some opened schools in several communities and then traveled from one to the other giving courses. Others simply traveled from town to town offering temporary classes.

While men like Rush, Barber and Porter treated elocution with a scientific respect that made contributions to a basic understanding of speech, many of their great mass of followers did not. Some made elocution into a cult with little of the soundness of learning. Often they completely ignored the intellectual content of the spoken word and indicated that only the formation of the sound counted. Giles W. Gray, Professor Emeritus of Speech at Louisiana State University, says: "It became more and more a kind of art form in itself. People became not readers, but elocutionists—practitioners of the art of delivery with nothing to deliver." Professor Gray speaks of a kind of mysticism that developed around this unusual movement as it went down in disrepute. He says: "... much of the elocution of the late nineteenth and early twentieth centuries degenerated into statue-posing, bird calls, and imitation of children—probably not all of which was imitation."

EMBRACE OF THE WRITTEN WORD

The rise, decline and fall of elocution coincides with the period in American education when the written word gained its current supremacy. The change to the visual medium was reflected downward in education and the old elementary-school oral-reading drills slowly gave way to the silent reading that we now know.

Not everyone liked the change. In his memoirs, the superintendent of schools at Salem, Massachusetts, William A. Mowry, wondered if the neglect of oral reading was right. "By the books in use from 1830 to 1860 and after," said the superintendent, "the directions ... (articulation, enunciation, pronunciation, vowels and consonants, accent, emphasis, inflections, tones and modulations and in some books many other topics) for training the voice were enforced in the daily lessons. Now much less attention is paid to these matters. The method today seems to be to read good literature, books by the best authors. Doubtless this improves thought and the written forms of expression, but it lacks the power of expressing that thought by the vocal organs. We have in these days 'Schools of Expression,' 'Schools of Oratory' and similar institutions by other names, but where do we find the same excellence of teaching tone and pitch, force and emphasis, articulation and pronunciation, as was common in the best schools a half century and more ago?"

DOMINATION AND REVOLT

The teaching of language by the turn of this century was well entrenched in the departments of English where the written word was dominant. Often disdain for the spoken word was demanded of English teachers. One who tried to instruct oral-language skills in a college English department might very well find himself labeled as a "crackpot elocution-ist," and seldom promoted.

English departments eventually were like quicksand for speech instruction. In numerous instances, when the teaching of public speaking, oratory, expression, elocution or whatever it might be called, was assigned to the English department, oral instruction would soon disappear completely from the school catalogue.

When the National Council of the Teachers of English was formed in 1911, its membership contained a number of teachers of public speaking who were not happy with their lot. They felt their only chance for academic survival was, in the words of Dartmouth College's J. M. O'Neill, ". . . the general deliverance of this work from English Department control." By 1915 O'Neill and sixteen other college and uni-versity teachers of public speaking had become charter members of the newly formed National Association of Aca-demic Teachers of Public Speaking. The organization, which became the present Speech Association of America, was clear evidence that the minority who taught oral skills were revolt-ing from the far more powerful majority who ran the na-tion's English departments.

From the revolt grew the departments of speech now found in most of our institutions of higher learning. In the half-century development of the new field of speech, consid-erable research has been conducted and a number of schol-arly journals have been established. The first Ph.D. in speech was granted in 1922 and the number has now risen to over 2,300, with forty different universities conferring the de-grees. At the same time some 18,000 masters degrees have been granted by 150 institutions.

"Teachers and scholars identified with the academic field of speech," says a statement prepared by the Speech Associa-tion of America, "label themselves in various ways: speech and linguistic scientists, speech clinicians, audiologists, rhetoricians, students of theater, teachers of speech. As scientists they seek to understand and describe speech behavior, and the process of communication. As humanists, they study the practical and artistic forms of discourse associated with the oral tradition of Western civilization. As teachers, they transmit the products of their study to students and help them develop effective, responsible, and artistic habits of communication."

A TURN TO TRADITION

The leaders of modern speech education think of themselves as inheritors of one of the finest cultural traditions in Western civilization. They feel that they have picked up the rhetorical traditions so ably started in America by men like John Quincy Adams and Edward T. Channing at Harvard, and Chauncey Allen Goodrich at Yale, all of whom drew upon the teachings of the ancients. And the modern speech leader rejects the latter nineteenth-century traditions that "shriveled in the hands of the less wise, less humane elocutionists." The Speech Association of America explains its roots in this way:

"Although its name is a coinage of this century, speech as a field of study grew from an academic tradition as old as the history of Western education. The study of the theory and practice of public discussion, under the name *rhetoric*, was a central concern of Greek, Roman, medieval, renaissance and early modern education. Subjects allied to rhetoric also flourished in the Western educational tradition: argumentative dialogue and logical inquiry, usually called *dialectic;* literature which was inseparably linked to rhetoric; and speculative inquiry into the nature and function of language."

CONTINUED CONFLICT

But the country's teachers of speech are not nearly as well established in the academic kingdom as they feel they ought to be. The old rift between them and the teachers of English is a continuing conflict, with the speech people usually on the defensive. For instance, one recent spring in California the State Council on Education was about to delete speech as part of teacher certification in the humanities, when the Western Speech Association came to the defense of its calling and successfully argued down the action. Pennsylvania teachers of speech have complained to their professional association that when they apply for certification it often requires two or three letters in defense, not of themselves, but of their profession.

"Repeated attacks on speech by school administrators," writes the editor of *Today's Speech,* "the cancellation of courses whenever pressure for new emphasis arises, be it for math, science or football, the belief that 'anybody can teach speech,' or the shunting of speech in the category of 'special courses' betrays a lack of knowledge on the part of guilty persons, rather than a deliberate attempt to harass speech teachers."

And here, from another professional speech journal, is another statement of the modern plight of speech teaching: ". . . rhetoric has become the Peck's Bad Boy of the schoolroom, crowned with a dunce cap and hunched over on a stool in the corner, while scholars of the learned disciplines tiptoe by with averted eyes and sanctimonious looks. . . . Some vested-rights educators arrogate rhetoric to the bargain basement of pedagogical knacks and quacks, and others pronounce oratory and debate as dirty words."

What hurts a speech man most is to find the word, *rhetoric,* stripped of its oral connotation and set forth as a discipline rooted in the written form of language. In a letter published in *The Speech Teacher,* a University of Connecticut Assistant Professor of Speech, Haig A. Bosmajian, wants to know: "Have the teachers of speech handed over to the English Department the task of teaching rhetoric...?" He then gives the names of several new books: *The Rhetoric-Reader, A College Rhetoric, Reading for Rhetoric, Logic and Rhetoric, Modern Rhetoric, An American Rhetoric* and *A Rhetoric Casebook.* Then asks the speech professor pointedly: "Titles of speech texts? No, these are titles of 'Freshman Composition texts'.... One can appreciate the university students' bewilderment as to who is really teaching rhetoric. The confusion has gone so far that an English Department Chairman demanded, upon hearing that the Speech Department was planning to add a course called 'History of Rhetorical Criticism,' that 'Rhetorical' be changed to 'Speech.' His demand was honored and that Speech Department is without its 'rhetoric.' How has such a situation come about?"

SHADES OF ELOCUTION

One answer is that the teachers of speech—and they frequently cite this reason—still work in the shadows of elocution. Moreover the trees that cast these shadows are far from dead. Both in and out of the academic world today one can find many teachers and writers of books, courses, articles and other tracts whose approach to oral language is not far from the elocutionary practices that brought the movement down awash in pseudoscience. The elocutionist's modern counterpart goes to the public with well-stocked advertising budgets and oral gimmicks which offer personal power, hyperconfidence, and raises in pay. These practitioners are the bane of the scholarly men of speech who base their teachings on oral methods and skills that are strongly oriented toward improvement of the intellectual development of speech, while the technical, mechanical side is seen as a supporting factor. But while deploring the gimmick vendors, the academic teachers of speech are often hit, like innocent bystanders, by criticism that is really thrown at these modern-day elocutionists. In many academic halls, the speech teacher, regardless of his intellectual integrity, is suspect.

"Almost every member of our profession can testify from personal acquaintance," says Carroll C. Arnold, Associate Professor of Speech at Cornell University, "that there are those in our schools and colleges who, though willing to admit speech to the educational scullery, would deny it the more dignified associations of the academic parlor. To such persons speech seems an educational 'extra.' When their lines of thought and argument are traced, these critical attitudes are usually found to be rooted in one of two general convictions or premises:

"Speech is a special subject, chiefly remedial or artistic, and is therefore, important only to the seriously deficient and the especially gifted;

"or

"Speech is not a true subject at all but an assortment of special activities which may be properly and adequately provided outside the regular academic schedule."

CONTINUED CURRICULUM CURB

The effects of such attitudes are particularly evident in the nation's secondary schools, and very much more so in our primary schools. For example, a study conducted in the 1960s surveyed the speech education in the public-secondary schools of the intermountain states (Arizona, Colorado, Idaho, Montana, Nevada, New Mexico, Utah and Wyoming). Of the 584 schools responding to the survey less than half said they offered their students a speech program. Those who did, however, revealed through a questionnaire that the amount and quality of such training left much to be desired. Speech was not generally a required subject and only 12.93 per cent of the students in the schools offering speech registered for it. Most often the Department of English seemed to be much in control of the meager offerings and teachers assigned to speech were usually English majors with a minor in speech. Their professional organizations were not those devoted to the spoken word and what they taught as speech was but the thinnest part of the discipline. Public speaking was the foremost subject and the teachers, like last century's elocutionists, laid great stress on the mechanics and personal benefits of speech, rather than stressing it as a skill central to the success or failure of man's most used, most important communication. Other surveys in other parts of the country have borne out this one.

The Speech Association of America keeps repeating that attention to oral language development is necessary from the elementary grades through the nation's institutions of higher learning. Lack of attention to this field, says the association, is a serious matter to the growth and use of knowledge through education. In a statement whose beginning is charitable to fellow educators, the professional group says: "The American educational system recognizes the importance of speech instruction, but it has not decided upon the amount and kind that should be generally provided for the common education of Americans. Despite massive evidence to the contrary, the assumption that speaking skill can be expected to develop as a by-product of instruction in reading and writing seems still to be prevalent. In too many schools, instruction in speech is represented only in extracurricular endeavor."

In nearly all the grades of junior high and high school, says the Speech Association, courses of instruction in the English language arts are found, and while it has been assumed that such training adequately covers the oral side of language it can hardly be true, for "as a rule teachers prepared within college departments of English have received little instruction in speech and language behavior and the arts of public discussion." And here are the consequences as outlined by the association:

"Innumerable graduates of the common schools have practically no knowledge of speech behavior and the arts of communication, only the superficial acquaintance with any of the 'literature' of public address and discussion, and no experience at all in rhetorical analysis and appraisal. Large numbers of graduates face a variety of situations requiring ready speech with powers far under their abilities. Such an attenuated and unbalanced treatment of the study of language and the development of language skills is a most serious problem in American education. Teachers of speech and English must recognize their related problems in the curriculum in the English language arts and confront them co-operatively."

THE VACUUM

Meanwhile, a vacuum is left in that part of education dealing with human communication. The graduates of our schools lack the skills and experience in oral language that many soon find are badly needed in modern life. Into this vacuum come adult educators of many descriptions—some good, others no more than quacks—who take over a task left unattended, though it should have been the business of our teachers from the kindergarten up.

Even at its best, the belated mending job in oral education by no means remedies the failure of America's schools to deal with our most used, most important mode of expression.

VII

The Choice
of Sense or Sound

ONE TIME IN Baltimore a nervous adult student stepped before fellow classmates to give his first talk in a course that, among other benefits, was supposed to teach him to speak well. But before he could start, the fear that the training was to eliminate overcame the poor man and he collapsed to the floor in a faint. The instructor rushed up to administer first aid, but first he turned to the astonished class and proclaimed: "Within a month this man will be speaking from the stage with confidence." It came true, of course.

This anecdote is one of hundreds testifying to the success of the confident instructor, the late Dale Carnegie, and his famous courses. A St. Paul, Minnesota, man, for example, is said to have taken the Dale Carnegie course to help his nerves, and near the end of the training, he appeared before his classmates, rolled up his sleeves and revealed how a skin rash had been cured. A housewife graduate found that she finally had the confidence to introduce herself to a neighboring housewife whom she had avoided for two years for fear that she wouldn't know what to talk about in their first meeting. A Des Moines, Iowa, meat salesman, holder of the same job for forty-two years, had tried for five years before taking the Dale Carnegie training to place an order with the Iowa

State Fair, but on the next attempt his newly learned approach closed a sale of 100,000 hot dogs.

The Dale Carnegie Course in Effective Speaking and Human Relations is given in 1,077 United States cities and towns by a parent company, Dale Carnegie & Associates, which also offers a special course for women, under the guidance of Carnegie's widow, Dorothy Carnegie, and another special course designed for sales people. Students, who pay from $135 to $185, come from all walks of life and educational levels. Along with the bakers and barbers the Carnegie people point out that trainees come from such institutions as Harvard, Cornell and Princeton. The list even includes Earl McGrath, former U.S. Commissioner of Education. But mostly the celebrated graduates are leaders in industry.

The Dale Carnegie course takes 14 weeks with one session per week. The course literature includes an assignment book, pamphlets, and Dale Carnegie's published works: *How to Win Friends and Influence People, Public Speaking and Influencing Men in Business,* and *How to Stop Worrying and Start Living.*

The all-male instructors, trained by the Carnegie organization, are said to be "a combination of teacher, psychologist, actor, stage manager, master salesman, raconteur, cheerleader and counselor." Less than half hold college degrees, with about two per cent holding doctorates. Many work in other jobs besides the Carnegie instructorship.

The teachers stress learning by practice. In the first session, students immediately make short speeches that demonstrate how to do something, like changing a tire, or eating with chopsticks. The early assignments are supposed to accomplish one of the course's most advertised benefits: "Control Fear and Worry."

The fifth night, a course landmark, is labeled "Coming Out of Your Shell," and designed to shock members "out of their inhibitions and repressions." The instructor asks stu-

dents to remove sharp or breakable objects like rings, wrist-
watches or eyeglasses, and he checks to see if anyone has a
heart condition. The session takes tremendous vigor. Each
student speaker is given a rolled up newspaper with which to
pound the speaker's table as he talks on a subject that can
raise his blood pressure. Meanwhile classmates heckle the
speaker and attempt to drown him out.

Dale Carnegie once said: "I discovered this horseplay
would do more to help people develop ease and naturalness
on their feet than any other method I ever tried. So we have
been using it for over forty years. If each member will enter
into this session with real spirit, he will get a lot of benefits
from it." A Carnegie tale from Minnesota tells of a man who
lost his mind as he slapped walls and windows, and tried
striking his fellow students, until he had to be physically re-
strained. The effort, said his instructor, was worth it because
the man in his brief, uncontrolled swatting session, reached
"the turning point in his struggle to gain self-confidence."

Another enervating session, the eighth, is designed to in-
fuse enthusiasm. First the student is physically warmed up,
until his "color reddens and his breathing increases," with
calisthenics or instructor-devised exercises like cranking an
old car or sawing wood. When properly pepped up, the student gives a two-minute enthusiastic talk on enthusiasm. "If
you began, four weeks ago, to use *five* times as much enthusiasm as usual in your daily life," says the Red Book of course
assignments, "believe me, you will have a story to tell us
tonight."

In session ten Carnegie customers give the "fear and
worry" speech, where they unburden themselves, and ". . .
there's often enough anguish unlimbered to fuel a soap opera
for months."

In session eleven's "crashing through" drill, students exercise their lungs with boisterous mimicry. In the "Joe Louis
drill" they imitate Harry Balough, the man who used to in-

troduce the famous fighter at Madison Square Garden without the benefit of a microphone.

The last three sessions give the students a chance to make some short talks, like a speech of introduction and an unprepared impromptu talk. As true with all assignments, these talks are exceptionally short. Most are only 60 or 90 seconds long, and in a couple of instances they may run for a full two minutes.

A last reminder in the assignment book, one that is repeated over and over throughout the course, is to turn in the names of friends who might be interested in taking the same training.

SPEECH IN DEMAND

More than a million people have completed the "Dale Carnegie Course in Effective Speaking and Human Relations." But they by no means represent all the people interested in improved speech; it is one of America's most popular adult-education courses, in schools, colleges and private schools like Carnegie's. People also buy how-to-do-it literature about better speech, so America's publishers recognize that popular better-speaking books, like cookbooks, are long-term sellers.

This widespread desire for speech improvement, a reflection of the vacuum left by America's schools in the area of spoken language, is frequently filled with a kind of speech education seriously questioned in the academic realms of the spoken word. It is often oriented toward technique with much too little emphasis on content. Hence the training is concerned with the mechanics of delivery and not with the intellectual development of the spoken word. For instance, this approach was emphasized by a single sentence repeated several times by a man conducting a Dale Carnegie demonstration session that I attended in New York. "The ability to

express an idea," he stressed, "is as important as the idea itself." This "rule," he claimed, came from Aristotle.

CONTENT OR TECHNIQUE

The ancient Greek philosopher has been followed by
many American teachers of rhetoric and oratory, but their
general interpretation of Aristotle has usually been opposite
the so-called "rule." One such devotee was John Quincy
Adams, a man intensely concerned that his Harvard students
dealt in ideas in their oratorical preparations; meanwhile he
all but neglected the teaching of speech delivery. Another
was Emerson; on the subject of eloquence, he made clear that
ideas were more important than their expression. He said
that the effective orator had to keep "his feet ever on a fact,"
that: "Fame of voice or of rhetoric will carry people a few
times to hear a speaker; but they soon begin to ask, 'What is
he driving at?' and if this man does not stand for anything, he
will be deserted."

A great modern teacher of speech, the late William Norwood Brigance, frequently referred to Aristotle. He told his
students, "Effective speaking is not merely a technique and
nothing more. It is very much more. It is also an intellectual
discipline. Now exactly what is an 'intellectual discipline?' *It
is developing the ability to produce and manage ideas.*" He
emphasized that to speak well one must first find sound
ideas—a task that requires far more than the speaking itself.
"This is old knowledge to experienced speakers," said Professor Brigance, "and as early as 336 B.C. Aristotle listed twenty-
eight sources of ideas that could be found in the speaker's
mind. Yet each new generation must learn it anew—that ideas
must be stalked with persistence and patience."

One of Brigance's most respected contemporaries, Elbert
W. Harrington, Dean of the College of Liberal Arts at the
University of North Dakota, places the stress on ideas over

mechanics when he explains, "Original speechmaking and discussion call for the evaluation of data, the establishment of relationships among ideas and a recognition of the strength and weakness of assumptions which underlie ideas or whole systems of thought. —Good speech is fundamentally a thinking process."

A MARKET FOR SECRET FORMULAS

But most graduates of an American education have never encountered such explanations. Their ideas of good speech are not likely to include the intellectual side of oral improvement, but are likely to coincide with what Dr. Brigance warned his students against: "bag-of-tricks magic." The reasons for good speech, in this view of it, have less to do with oral understanding, than with personal development. In the popular view, building good speech depends only on the acquisition of an easily understood, but secret formula whose application requires only a "short" course that demands little labor, mental or otherwise. With this formula the individual's tongue turns to silver, along with a host of other attractive human bonuses. Fear disappears. Human relations improve. Friendships widen. Self-confidence increases. Take-home pay rises. The promotion dam breaks. And on and on.

This idea of improved speech is marketed in America to individuals, and, for considerable sums, to industry and government. Those who peddle the secrets of speech sell to the leading names of American business whose employees take the courses. Not all the training, of course, is poorly done, for some well-qualified people, especially from the academic field of speech, are hired by business to teach employees. But one can hardly scratch the surface of such education without finding a heavily technique-oriented kind of training, low on concern for content—which, of course, is what many adult students are seeking.

Waldo W. Braden, Professor and Chairman of the Department of Speech at Louisiana State University, tells of teaching an evening adult-speech-education class where sat an unhappy salesman who followed the assignments with obvious lack of enthusiasm. Finally, his disappointment was too much to contain and he asked Professor Braden, "When do we get to the *tricks?*" When told there were none, he quit the course.

"Yes, I object to the short courses which promise not only to teach effective communication," says Professor Braden, "but also promise to develop concentration, memory, personality, charm and vitality. Some even throw in how to be a master salesman as well as how to be the life of the party. I dislike to have speech listed with driver training, first aid and speedball."

But this is the level where one locates much of the adult-speech training. Following is some evidence of the intellectually poor grade of speech training in much adult education:

One of the nation's largest insurance companies gives its employees a nine-session course in "effective speaking" dominated by simple admonitions, such as: stand erect, act confident though you don't feel confident, look at your audience, relax and be natural, start in a conversational tone, begin in an interesting manner, speak loudly enough for all to hear, concentrate on getting the message across, be enthusiastic so your audience can be enthusiastic, be sincere, finish strongly and don't thank your audience. The intellectual development of a speech is pretty much limited to a couple of thin hints: know your subject thoroughly by having ten times more information than the talk will use, and make points clear by illustrating them with examples, stories and facts.

One of the nation's largest industrial corporations uses a twenty-page speech booklet of cartoons which are not "fogged up" with too much reading materials, only a few secret methods. "Stand up straight and look 'em in the eye," says method number one. "If you look confident they'll think you're confident." Second method: "Don't mumble, apologize and mop your brow. Don't grin foolishly." And the third item: "Dress neatly, but not flashily. They came to hear *you*, not your necktie. If you look sloppy, they'll expect a sloppy talk. Clothes and a haircut may not make a man, but they'll make *him* look like one."

In the booklet's conclusion are some final dos and don'ts. Hands out of the pockets! it warns, and then helpfully explains that if the speaker cannot do so, he might try having his pockets sewn up. Don't rub your nose, scratch your head, pull your ear, polish your glasses, smoke, chew gum or hem and haw. The reader is given a final, forceful formula. Starting with his left foot pointed directly at the audience and his right foot parallel to the audience, he is to pivot on the right heel and rotate the toe back and forth, between its right angle position and one parallel to the other foot. "From this alert stance you can give a forceful speech," says the corporation booklet, "and you'll find it keeps you from rocking back and forth." The publication says nothing about the speech content that is to strike the listeners so forcefully as the speaker waves his toes.

A speech improvement book has been published especially for the "technical man." Recognizing his reliance on mathematics, the authors define "practical speaking" in algebraic equations each of which summarizes a chapter. For example, one equation is:

$$BVFD = \frac{BA}{PFDGI.}$$

The interpretation is that to *Be Visually Forceful* and *Direct* equals putting *Purpose, Force, Directness, Genuineness,* and *Interpretation* into your *Bodily Activity.*

Another formula-type speech book was brought out by the same publisher offering readers "the new Speech-O-Gram technique" designed for "persuasive public speaking." The Speech-O-Gram takes the pain out of speech preparation by providing sort of "instant" or "dehydrated" talks for many occasions at which a reader of the book could rise to his feet whenever beckoned and give a speech that would appear to be extemporaneous. In this book the reader also receives memory aids, tricks to counter stage fright and other helpful hints for successful speaking.

LOW LEVEL TOPICS

The mechanics-oriented speech teachers are confronted with one persistent fact: the students have to talk about something. This might be the opportunity for dealing with the important content development of oral language but again the student is offered easy-do-it formulas, most of which are notably abstract. The formulas talk about starting speeches with something that will "set the listeners on fire." They overdo the business of telling students to illustrate with stories and examples. Brevity is a sacred rule, whether an idea takes time to develop or not. Students are practically ordered to talk about something they know, thereby discouraging subjects which might require some research; by following this rule, say the vendors of popular speech education, the student has, in effect, prepared for many, many years (it matters little that such personally known subjects can more often than not be the most irrelevant, boring topics in the world). The easy-does-it teachers often offer intellectually vacuous lists of topics for various assignments, as a few suggested subjects from one popular course will illustrate: "How I cured a cold." "An unforgettable experience with 'puppy love.'" "I had forgotten my wallet." "I was 'mad as a wet hen.'" "My

experience at the circus." "A picnic that I will always remember." And "I ran out of gasoline."

COSTLY MISCONCEPTIONS

Hundreds of millions of dollars have been spent by American adults and their employers on this kind of speech education whose intellectual aims seem not much higher than play-
school. That this can happen is a product of our general
educational neglect of the spoken word. Millions of Americans, including many with extensive educations, have practically no understanding of what is shadow and substance in
oral language training.

At Pennsylvania State University, Harold P. Zelko, who
has been a leader in trying to improve business and government communication, outlined four widely held misconcep-
tions which have helped promote "a philosophy of speech
training based on mechanics and techniques."

1. SPEECH IS PURELY A SKILL

The most apparent parts of speech, voice and bodily
movement, are easiest to deal with; therefore, the shallowest
speech training is likely to be limited to them. "Actually,"
says Professor Zelko, "the oral communication process involves a man's greatest combination of achievements as a
human being: his ability to think, reason and express himself
understandingly to others. The speech skill must start with
the thinking process, and the actual physical act of speaking
is only what the other person hears and sees of the speaker.
We must also keep in mind that we are using the word
'thought' very broadly to include . . . feelings, emotions and
attitudes, all of which only makes the process more complex

and takes us even farther from the misconception that speaking is purely a skill."

2. EFFECTIVE SPEAKING IS CHIEFLY TECHNIQUE

This tries to formulize the complicated speech act into a set of all-inclusive rules, which is practically impossible. The mechanics of speech, says Professor Zelko, "are secondary to the more important factors of attitude, understanding of others, awareness of the social relationships in the speech situation, and an understanding of the complexities in the communication process as a whole. '

"Of course we want to suggest to the speaker how he should best use these tools, but the average practical speech-training course should spend little time having him practice the mechanics of doing this. The fundamental reason is that one will use his voice and body effectively if he is properly animated and has the proper attitude. Modern speech textbooks are therefore very much social-psychological in their emphasis rather than technique centered."

3. THE EFFECTIVE SPEAKER IS AN ORATOR

Here is a shadow of last century when speech was marked with "oratorical qualities" that depended heavily upon the mechanical parts of speaking, a booming voice, sweeping gestures, and planned poses. They were effective in their day for catching the attention of audiences that were largely uninformed, but today's listeners are not likely to respect florid oratory, for it runs counter to our growing respect for learning and knowledge. Still the technique-oriented courses often emphasize such mechanical factors because they can be easily and graphically presented.

4. EFFECTIVE SPEAKERS ARE BORN

Good speech is not a matter of inheritance, for all human beings, unless they suffer certain physical or mental drawbacks, learn to speak and the quality of learning varies, even in its most natural, unplanned form. The process can be picked up at most any stage of life and improved upon. Professor Zelko points out, the benefits of good speech training are not limited to the making of an effective speaker. "[That] it can equip a man to go out and make a speech is obvious," says the Pennsylvania educator, "but the extent it can develop the whole man is not as much realized. Yet the reason that good speech training can do this is clear, for the way a man speaks is the expression of his whole self. When he improves his ability to do this he feels himself grow as a person in a way that no other training course can accomplish. Training effective speaking thus develops not only his ability to make a speech, it reinforces his ability to communicate orally in all situations where he finds himself face-to-face with other people." Also, speech training oriented in the direction of its intellectual content can hardly avoid helping a person's ability to think.

A CONTENT–ORIENTED MINIMUM

The Pennsylvania educator believes that a course aimed at the intellectual-content improvement of speech, as well as developing the vocal techniques that it might require, should take a minimum of twenty class hours, preferably divided into ten equal sessions. He offers some general advice for building such a course:

The subject matter should move from the problems of shaping attitudes, understanding the communication process and the people involved to the teaching and application of the time-tested principles of planning, organizing, analyzing, developing, motivating listeners and communicating with others. The spoken practice to accompany this training should proceed from short, easy assignments to longer, more difficult ones.

Unlike so many popular courses where only praise and no criticism is offered, Professor Zelko recommends that everyone participate in the evaluation and criticism of everyone else. In the process, good listening should be emphasized and put to work to insure that the critical participation is constructive.

He also recommends that attention in a business speech course be paid to the kind of interpersonal communication that occurs between two people. Practice here can be furnished through role playing with two people or small groups.

Finally the speech educator says the instructor should engage in a minimum of lecturing and should depend on a good text. But finding the right text for a business course in speech is not necessarily an easy task. Most texts of substance are directed toward the college undergraduate, and even those which say they are aimed at business classes are basically the same college texts. "They are usually long, pedantic, chiefly public speaking-oriented," explains the speech teacher, "and with some minor reference or adaptation to the business world to make them seem more palatable for business courses." He has called on his colleagues in the field of speech to provide more texts suitable for the business world.

MENDING AND PATCHING

Regardless of design, today's adult speech training amounts to a mending job for patching up the hole left by general education's neglect of the spoken word. If and when our schools take over this task, so rightfully theirs, adult courses in speech, if needed at all, are bound to rise to higher intellectual levels. The purveyors of magic formulas, tricks, and mechanical techniques would then find it more difficult to sell their wares, for speech education in the right place at the right time would help expose the brands of training which approach quackery.

Meanwhile, the leaders of American management training, many of whom now support the shallowest efforts for oral-language improvement, have a chance to upgrade today's adult speech education by limiting their expenditures to courses where the cultivating and care of ideas is central to good and responsible communication. Examples of this are already found in some companies, associations and training firms. One case is the American Management Association's course entitled "Executive Action," which is described by the organization as a course concerned with the "ways to translate ideas into plans and programs ... to convert thoughts and decisions into action and results." Also a large number of industries seeking help with their problems in oral communication have wisely turned to the universities for help from the speech profession.

The Speech Association of America, with headquarters in New York's Statler Hilton Hotel, is a good general source of information for anyone seeking help in speech education. The following is a statement from the Association about its services:

"The Speech Association of America is a professional and scholarly organization that is devoted to the improvement of speech education in all of its dimensions. Its membership is composed principally of teachers of speech in the nation's schools, colleges and universities. The Association does not operate a school, nor does it engage in any form of direct instruction. Through its publications, conventions, placement service and other membership activities, it strives to promote a high caliber of speech instruction from kindergarten (and 'preschool') through graduate studies and adult education.

"The Association does not recommend particular schools or particular teachers of speech; it does recommend to the lay public that competent advice on speech problems can be secured through college and university speech departments. Many such departments operate clinics with out-patient services for persons with communicative disorders, and many provide superior instruction in public speaking through their extension or adult-education programs. A number of high schools offer excellent evening classes in speech. SAA members frequently serve as communication consultants to business, industry and the government.

"Persons who are not engaged in speech education per se but who have a strong interest in oral communication may find it profitable to affiliate with the Speech Association of America."

A FINAL FORMULA

There is a short sentence of advice—a formula, if you want to call it that—which might serve as a useful guide to anyone seeking oral education of quality. It comes from Lewis Carroll's *Alice in Wonderland*. The Duchess has a thought for Alice about communication and she says: "Take care of the sense and the sounds will take care of themselves."

VIII

A Lesson
Unheeded

AN ARDENT STUDENT and master of the spoken word wrote the following paragraphs:

"The speaker may . . . treat the same subject as that of a book, yet if he is a great and ingenious popular speaker he will hardly twice repeat in the same manner one and the same subject matter and material. He will always let himself be carried by the great masses in such a manner that he senses just those words that he needs in order to speak to the hearts of his respective listeners. But if he errs, no matter how slightly, he has always before him the living correction . . . he is able to read from the expressions of his listeners, firstly, whether they *understand* what he speaks, secondly, whether they are able to *follow what has been said,* and thirdly, in how far he has convinced them of the *correctness* of what has been said. If he sees—firstly—that they do not understand him, then he will become so primitive and clear in his explanation that even the least intelligent is bound to understand him, if he feels—secondly—that they are not able to follow him, then he will build up his ideas so carefully and slowly that even the weakest among them all does not remain behind any longer, and—thirdly—as soon as he guesses that they do not seem to be convinced of the correctness of what he has said he will repeat this so often and in so many new examples, he himself will bring in their objections which he feels although they have not been uttered, and he will refute them and disperse till finally even the last group of an opposition, merely by its attitude and its expressions, lets him recognize its capitulation in the face of his argument.

"It seems that in the morning and even during the day men's will power revolts with highest energy against an attempt at being enforced under another's will and another's opinion. In the evening, however, they succumb more easily to the dominating force of a stronger will. For truly every such meeting presents a wrestling match between two opposed forces. The superior oratorical talent of a domineering apostolic nature will now succeed more easily in winning . . . people who themselves have in turn experienced a weakening of their force of resistance in the most natural way, than people who still have full command of the energies of their minds and their will power."

These striking ideas about the power of speech were written by modern history's worst demagogue, Adolf Hitler, who firmly believed that all "really great historical changes" were brought about by the spoken word, and only "accompanied" by the written word. He expresses these thoughts in *Mein Kampf*, Volume II, Chapter 6, the second half of which is entitled "The Significance of the Spoken Word."

DEVOTION TO THE SPOKEN WORD

Of all their propaganda efforts, the least known in America but the most important to Hitler and his propaganda chieftain, Joseph Goebbels, was that concerned with swaying and holding the people of Germany to the Nazi way of thinking. For this task they chose what both believed to be an unmatched weapon, the spoken word.

Goebbels once asked: "Did Christ write books or did he preach? Did Mohammed write intellectual essays or did he go to the people and tell them what he wanted? When Lenin came from Zurich to Petersburg, did he go from the station to the study and write a book or did he not instead speak before thousands?" He answered, saying: ". . . there is no difference between the speaker and the politician. One can prove in history that the great politician was also a great speaker: Napoleon, Caesar, Alexander, Mussolini, Lenin, you can name who you want." Above all, Goebbels named Hitler, "the first to use speech as a tool to make history." Indeed, when the Third Reich's most serious defeats were beginning and German morale was dropping, the propaganda chieftain seemed of the opinion that the troubles could be remedied by a good speech from his master. In his diary for November 8, 1943, Goebbels noted: "It is high time the Fuehrer delivers a long speech in public to instill courage in the German people."

AN UNLEARNED LESSON

The story of speech in Nazi Germany offers a startling lesson of how important it is for a society to be concerned with the proper use of the spoken word in the realm of leadership. Events of recent years in America reveal that we have obviously not learned this lesson. Today there are striking parallels to what was found in Germany as Hitler came to power. The Hitlerian story of speech is therefore worth reviewing in more detail.

In post–World War I, Germany was recognized as one of the world's best educated nations, yet Hitler saw an intellectual weakness and exploited it. The future dictator recognized that German leadership was largely supported by writing, while great orators did not exist. In this disparity Hitler found his avenue to power. While journalists and other intellectuals worked with the least powerful tool of communication, the written word, he would capture the people's minds

with the most powerful form, the spoken word. Thus he
would win over the masses and fill them with the fires of
emotion to battle for the causes of National Socialism. As we
all know, it worked.

Hitler worshiped the spoken word mainly for its raw
power to move masses of people by its sound and the setting
in which it was uttered. Conversely the Fuehrer found writers the lowest form of life. He called them "the average
sparrow-brain of a German scribbler." They were "knights of
the pen," "bourgeois simpletons," and "bourgeois wisecrack-
ers." When writers went to the people, said Hitler, they were
pitifully lacking in anything other than an expository effort.
"... the bourgeois scribbler, who steps out of his study before
the masses," said the contemptuous Hitler, "is sickened
merely by their fumes and therefore faces them helplessly
also with the written word."

The writer forever works in the dark, said the Nazi
leader, for he really "does not know his readers at all." He
concluded: "For this reason he will, from the beginning not
aim at a certain crowd before his eyes, but he will keep his
arguments on quite general lines. By this he loses, to a certain
degree, psychological finesse, and consequently suppleness. In
general, therefore, a brilliant speaker will still be able to
write better than a brilliant writer will be able to speak, unless he trains himself continuously in this art. To this he must
add that the mass of people is lazy in itself, that they lazily
remain within the course of old habits and that by themselves
they do not like to take up anything written unless it corre-
sponds to what one believes oneself, and furnishes what one
hopes for. Therefore a pamphlet with a certain tendency will
in most cases only be read by people who themselves must be
counted on its side."

This contempt for the writer was balanced by fervent
admiration for great orators, but to find them, Hitler had to
point to the speakers of other nations, even to the countries

he most hated. One of his more admired orators was England's David Lloyd George. In *Mein Kampf* Hitler scoffs at a German writer's analysis of Lloyd George's World War I speeches which said they were "intellectually and scientifically inferior," and "hackneyed and obvious products." "Later," said Hitler, "I personally obtained some of these speeches in the form of a small booklet and I had to laugh loudly at the fact that a normal German knight of the pen had no understanding of these psychological masterpieces of influencing the soul of the masses. This man judged these speeches exclusively according to the impression that they left on his own conceit while the great English demagogue had directed them exclusively at exercising the greatest possible influence on the mass of his listeners and in the widest sense on the entire lower English people. Looked at from this viewpoint, the speeches of this Englishman were the most wonderful achievements, as they gave proof of an actually astounding knowledge of the soul of the greatest layers of the people. Their effect, then, was a telling one."

MOBILIZATION OF SPEAKERS

With Hitler as their model, thousands of Germans were enlisted as official party speakers to wield the power of the spoken word across Germany. Their service began with a vast speakers' training program offered in all of thirty-nine districts designated by the National Socialist party.

The Nazi speakers had it drilled into them that "speech is the most beautiful and most effective means of national leadership," that it is "the strongest force to awaken faith, harden conviction, to destroy degeneration and to pull the masses from the old ways of thinking over to the street of new hopes." Successful graduates became "the living media" between the Nazis and the people, and later between the party and the government and the people.

"No nation of people," says a student of this movement, Ross Scanlon, "even among the true believers of Democracy, ever cultivated the power of the spoken word with more devotion and zeal than did the Nazis of Germany during their short history. Their literature on the techniques of propaganda teems with tributes to the role of the speaker."

TOTALLY TECHNIQUE

The Nazi leaders hardly cared *what* their speakers said providing it did one thing, which was, in Goebbels' words, "mobilize the masses and get them to march disregarding their personal advantages, and even under the acceptance of death and danger."

"I do not go into a meeting hall," said Goebbels, "to find intellectual revelations, but in order to transmit to others what I have realized is right." The model, as always, was Hitler. "His speeches," said Goebbels, "completely lack that irritating tone of superior wisdom so characteristic of the so-called speeches of learned minds."

A foundation block in the training was the teaching of enthusiasm, a quality that official Nazi speakers had to display to transmit it to their listeners. The orator's goal under all circumstances was to produce enthusiastic action in favor of the National Socialist movement and he was expected to carry out the mission though he sacrificed "time, health, and material values." More and more was expected from the program as the Nazi reverses of the 1940s commenced. In 1942, for example, Goebbels put on the pressure for training so speakers could go forth in increasing numbers to explain the military reverses in Russia and Africa, and to rebuild sagging morale.

But none of these speakers could compare with the Fuehrer whose personal magnetism toward Germany's common people was strengthened by all the external techniques of spoken language. A leader of the Hitler Youth, Fred Casmir, now a teacher of speech in America, has frequently written of growing up in Nazi Germany. "One must remember," says Professor Casmir, who teaches at Los Angeles' Pepperdine College, "that Hitler was the first truly popular speaker in German history. His ascent was made even easier by the development of the radio which he used frequently and well. . . . Whenever that voice was heard, I observed that adults sat down, listened carefully, with complete absorption showing in their faces. . . . Sometimes the whole country would come to a standstill as the voice of the 'Fuehrer' boomed over the land through loudspeakers which had been set up everywhere."

The power of Hitler's speech, regardless of its content, was astonishing. "Looking back today," says Professor Casmir, "the frightening thing was the 'logic' with which everything Hitler said fitted into the pattern he himself had designed.

"As he [Hitler] and I became absorbed in the ideas which could 'save' my country, I was not really concerned that his words lacked clarity, that his sentence structure was poor, that he used poor grammar, and that his voice was something less than pleasant. All this added to my concept of a man who was completely absorbed in truly important matters.

"When Hitler appeared, he spoke to me, in spite of the fact that I was only one of thousands."

PUBLIC SPEAKER'S PARADISE

Speech training in Nazi Germany not only included the mechanics of the speaker, but those of the meeting. Every gathering was carefully staged. Music was part of the ceremonies which always involved the flag and were handled in a military manner. Before the speaker appeared the music and

the ceremonies were used to heighten the listeners' emotions
and pave the way for a demagogic oration. Before Hitler's
public appearances his youth groups were subjected to hours
of marching, singing, and military drills that accomplished
the double purpose of building up an explosive emotional
climate, while exhausting the listeners so that they might be
all the more susceptible to the kind of logic which would
follow.

Eventually, as the Nazis' control of Germany solidified,
the party speakers always found their meetings in perfect
order. Previously they were told to expect to go home occasionally with a broken head, but by 1934 such acts of opposition had been squelched. On December 4 of that year *The New
York Times* said that Germany had become a "public speaker's
paradise," for a decree by Dr. Wilhelm Frick, the interior
minister, had flatly ordered an end to the heckling of Nazi
speakers, as well as questions and interruptions which might
stir up controversy.

SALUTE IL DUCE

Meanwhile, to the south Hitler had a formidable rival
when it came to the mechanics of meetings. Benito Mussolini
was another master orator whose public appearances were
preceded by unbelievable preparations. Consider the details
of just one such gathering:

Twenty-four hours prior to a Mussolini public address
people had no idea of the event. The first word came during
the day preceding the speech through rumors systematically
and strategically spread, followed by a poster appearing that
night on every street corner announcing the oration, but
only hinting at the subject. Morning newspapers then reflected the posters' incomplete message. In their morning
mail citizens of the city where il Duce was to speak received a
pink card saying they were expected to be at the scene of the

address at noon, although it did not state Mussolini's arrival time. The city's military personnel which included nearly every adult male, also received their orders to go to the square where the oration would be made. The people were further warned of il Duce's appearance by the pealing of church bells and by young boys (Ballilla Boys) who went out into the countryside beating drums to hail the rural citizens to come hear the speech.

While the great audience was being summoned, other strange preparations were under way to condition the crowds who would come to listen. City bus service was drastically reduced, or even stopped, so most people were forced to walk to the square. On the way and upon arrival they found public eating places closed. The dictator's rostrum was set on a high balcony, so that watching and listening to him would be a tiresome, neck-craning stint. By noon, when the speech was scheduled, the square was overcrowded, and the hot sun at its peak. Time went by and the dictator didn't come. As the people grew more and more uncomfortable they found that locks had made toilet facilities scarce. The general aim was to make the audience tired and irritable as they waited for the dictator who was always late. Usually he did not appear until after dark.

Eventually the crowd was treated to festivities, Fascist style. A half dozen or more brass bands played while bombers zoomed overhead in formation. The square was extensively decorated and surrounded by military units in full dress.

As it grew dark, bonfires were lit on the tops of nearby buildings and the great human mass was ringed with burning torches. With the eerie atmosphere, the tired, irritated, and hungry crowd's attention was eventually attracted to the balcony doors which slowly opened. In a moment two impressively dressed musketeers came out followed by Fascist dignitaries who stopped and turned toward the door, waiting in expectation as a great fanfare of trumpets was heard. Then through the door strutted Italy's second highest official, Secretary of the Fascist Party who stopped abruptly at the balcony rail and screamed: "Fascisti! Salute il Duce!" He then led the mass audience in the Fascist cheer: "Ejah! Ejah! Ejah! Alalah!"

Finally out strutted the bantam Mussolini to make a rousing oration filled with emotional appeals designed to channel the crowd's irritability toward whatever he was speaking against—and he was always against.

IS HE A GOOD MAN?

The Los Angeles speech professor who as a child experienced such spoken force under the German master has written: "To those of us who study and teach in the field of oral communication, Hitler stands as a warning of what can be done, even by an untrained speaker such as the 'Fuehrer' and a constant reminder that a good speaker must be a 'good man,' one who is pleasing to the gods [a paraphrase from Quintilian's *Institutio Oratoria*]. When one has decided what makes a man good, he is then faced with the problem of how one can adequately judge this goodness within a short period of time. Only when these insights are mastered, can we know that the future generations of men cannot be trapped by evil men such as Hitler.

"That Hitler was a great speaker cannot be doubted. The fact that he was the first real orator in German history made it more difficult for an untrained people to judge him correctly. Germany is justly paying for her mistakes, but she is not the first country nor will she be the last, where the ringing phrases of a dictator will first offer hope and then bring disaster."

CAN THE MASSES UNDERSTAND?

The history of Hitler's mad devotion to the spoken word —the results still fresh in mind—is an unparalleled case of a monumental and evil distortion warping a crucial form of communication which depends heavily upon oral language. It was described by Andrew Thomas Weaver, Professor of Speech at the University of Wisconsin, when he said: "Somehow [in a democratic society], working understandings between the gifted and creative leaders, on the one hand, and the great body of ordinary citizens on the other must be established and maintained. This is the central, perennial problem in a democracy. At long last, we are coming to appreciate the fact that it is not enough for technical experts and specialists to reach cooperative understandings with each other. Such rapport is essential, of course, but it is relatively easy to achieve. The real problem is how to get the masses to understand enough of what men of genius, the small creative minority, are about so that they will permit and encourage them to function in freedom and will be able to evaluate the solutions which these leaders make available to them. Such understanding is absolutely prerequisite to the safety and progress of our democratic society, and *we are still far short of having achieved it!*"

In pre-Nazi Germany, as Hitler understood so well, communication between "the gifted and creative leaders" and "the great body of ordinary citizens" was in poor order, and he replaced it with a brand of oral discourse that the German people in their post-war climate understood. Hitler was the evil man who understood the devious application of speech techniques. The German people on the other hand, good or bad, were unable as listeners to assess this man and his unprecedented demagoguery.

RIPE FOR A DEMAGOGUE

Today in America the communicative link that ties the people to their leadership is a tenuous line frequently battered by rhetorical storms which many fear may bring it down. The fear was pointedly expressed in the 50th Anniversary issue of the *New Republic,* by its regular political writer, signed T.R.B. "Under certain circumstances, never yet faced," wrote T.R.B., "this reporter has always felt that the U.S. would be a pushover for a demagogue. We are perhaps more vulnerable than any other big nation. Suppose we suffered defeat in war. Unthinkable? Tut, tut, Little Man; a century is a short time! Suppose the next A-1 demagogue should appear when times were really ripe for him, as they were not for Huey Long, who had to face a strong President; or McCarthy, who never could hit on any positive panacea to sell; or Senator Goldwater, whose pastoral demagoguery ran into the stone wall of prosperity.

"Will there be a conjunction of defeat, depression and demagogue? When these arrive together our defense will not be in written laws or a Constitution, I believe, but in an attitude of mind and instinct. Are we braced sufficiently strongly? Anyone who saw the Respectables wilt before McCarthy's attack knows that they are stuffed with straw. Always the timid, the bigots, the gullible turn to the strong man with simple answers. In Washington the demagogue has these opportunities: a Presidential candidate is often a relative newcomer to the political system; if and when he gets into the White House, he has the greatest concentration of power on earth; in an emergency even this elaborate power structure is traditionally stretched; and finally, the country tends to reach for a military man if one is available.

"... Is this a bogey? Maybe. Yet it leaves doubts to one

who has spent some years in Washington watching a tripartite government flounder about, frequently unable to locate the center of responsibility and often accompanied by a rise of public impatience."

If a confluence of today's fast-changing events should suddenly produce the river of emotions on which a demagogue could ride to power in America, public communication, so dependent on spoken language, would be tried as never before. Would we be prepared for such a test? Do America's habits of public speech indicate that we are intellectually capable to cope with the spoken techniques of a powerful demagogue? Do our listening habits reveal that the evil intents of such a man would be properly assessed and rejected by the masses he would seek as followers?

The answer, in all cases, is "No!" The state of the spoken word in America clearly shows that we did not learn a crucial lesson in speech from the downfall of Germany and Italy to evil orators.

IX

The Index
to Destiny

"THE STATE OF the mother tongue," says educator Jacques Barzun, "is the index of our control over destiny."

The truth of this statement is evident in a historical comparison of public speech and the civilization that went with it. From early Greece to the present, the quality of spoken language has usually been an indication of the rises and falls of civilization.

When the mechanical techniques of speech take the central role in public communication, things are usually not well for the civilization involved. When the concern for technique is replaced by that for the intellectual content of speech, the civilization is likely to be moving uphill. The peak appears to have been reached when speakers have carefully blended their attention for oral content with supporting concern for good but responsible oral methods. This was evident in the rise and fall of Greek and Roman civilizations. At their zenith the proper concern was shown for both content and the techniques necessary to support it. In the decline of these civilizations speech was honored for its form rather than substance. The great modern example of technique-oriented speech is the case of Nazi Germany.

One is quick to apply the index to the course of American speech since the founding of the Republic. Our early rhetoricians were intellectually oriented, sometimes almost to the complete disregard of speech methods. We saw it, for instance, in the teachings of John Quincy Adams at Harvard. But as America expanded through the pragmatic society of the frontier, speech veered toward elocution where technique became supreme and content was practically forgotten. In this century, the professional speech educator, turning to the early rhetoricians, has tried to balance his concern for ideas with one for responsible methods. Their efforts, however, have not been widely accepted.

Public speech in this half of the twentieth century is obsessed with technique to the disregard of content. It is most evident in that crucial area of communication between the leaders and the people of our society. In our highest public offices we find men who care little about *what* they say providing their words produce results for their causes. Among the millions who listen there are few prepared by education or experience to assess our public speech—and thereby demand that our leaders be men with ideas of quality.

This index to our destiny reveals an alarming acceptance of public speech that has both the ingredients and the audience for the rise of demagoguery—or at least the continual downgrading of society through poor leadership. If the index has any meaning at all, it cries out for attention to the predominantly oral communication between the leaders and the people.

Let's consider several timely examples of this communication while asking ourselves whether the talkers and listeners are concerned with the intellectual integrity of the spoken word or mainly with its techniques.

MANUFACTURING LEADERS

On September 13, 1952, the Republican Presidential candidate, General Dwight D. Eisenhower and his brother

Milton arrived in the New York studios of the Transfilm Corp. where they met an advertising man, Rosser Reeves, who was waiting with scripts for twenty-two spot announcements for television that the General was to read before the cameras. The twenty-two spots were all that were ready of fifty such announcements planned for the candidate's campaign that year. As the filming started, Reeves quickly recognized that General Eisenhower could work much faster than anticipated; all fifty scripts could be completed that day if they were available. So while the filming proceeded the advertising man sat at a nearby typewriter and hurriedly composed twenty-eight more spot announcements that the candidate narrated.

The General, cosmetically made up for the cameras, read the spots from large hand-lettered cards which allowed him to appear without eyeglasses, a requirement of the advertising man. As his reading caught up with Reeves' writing, the General had to wait in a hard chair for each new spot. The man to become the next President felt the day's doings were ludicrous. He shook his head frequently and said: "To think that an old soldier should come to this!"

During the campaign the spot announcements went on night and day across the nation with their tiny messages of a few seconds each. On one, for example, a voice asked the General about the high cost of living. The full answer: "My wife, Mamie, worries about the same thing. I tell her it's our job to change that on November fourth." The cost of putting the ultra-simple messages on the air ran to $1,500,000.

Though spot announcements had been used as early as 1936 on radio, the short, hurriedly prepared Eisenhower films were the first major effort using the candidate himself. As we know, they set a precedent and in today's election campaigns, one finds the sale of candidates generously mixed with the TV promotion of mayonnaise and pills for acid in the stomach.

A dozen years after the Eisenhower spots, the techniques had been well refined. As Robert Kennedy ran for the Senate against the New York incumbent Senator Kenneth Keating, $1,000,000 went into television to present the Democratic candidate in the state alone. Spot announcements took a large piece of that sum. Kennedy's advertising experts, concentrating upon image-building, followed him with cameras and sound equipment. On thousands and thousands of feet of film, they caught him in all kinds of spontaneous situations. From the massive stretch of celluloid, film technicians edited out some 100 commercials which varied from thirty-second spots to rather extensive films. In the world of political advertising they are looked upon as masterpieces for taking a candidate who had a lot against him and remaking him into another, but acceptable, image.

"Clearly," says Terry Smith, a New York reporter, "the chief problem the agency had to solve was the candidate's image as a Little League ogre. They had to warm up the merchandise. The job was not unlike that of getting tunafish moving after a botulism scare. Nobody disliked tuna: it just had to be proved it wouldn't hurt you.

"Senator Keating's commercials," says Smith, "by contrast, were traditional, almost folksy, productions. The principal spokesman was Senator Javits, who concluded most of them by thumping Keating on the back and urging viewers to 'vote for my teammate, Ken Keating.' In the background, a folk singer named Tedd Browne droned an original tune about the candidate that sounded like a dirge."

SQUELCH THAT DEBATE!

In such duels of technique, one seldom-stated purpose is to squelch the democratic debate about which Americans brag. Here, in evidence, is a statement by a large, politically engaged public-relations firm: "We do not believe it sound campaign practice to sponsor too many debates. They would make a forum for the opposition which would be difficult for them to secure otherwise, and they are easily stacked. This is particularly true of broadcasts to the public." Could stacking, in this case, mean that the opposition candidate might have more valid ideas than the public-relations firm's political client?

One *must* for political-campaign advertisers is the last-few-days saturation technique. Just before the voters go to the polls commercials are pumped out faster and faster bearing the most serious charges that can be leveled against the opposition. Thereby, debate is limited, for in the final furious hours, who has time for comparable rebuttals?

Cynicism is inherent in such technical assistance. "I think of a man in a voting booth who hesitates between two levers as if he were pausing between competing tubes of toothpaste in a drugstore . . ." said one advertising man quoted in a leading magazine. "The brand that has made the highest penetration on his brain will win his choice." Another advertising man blithely admitted that one of his client candidates did not have the mental equipment for the job he sought. His defense: "Let's consider this campaign clinically. After all, you don't criticize a brain surgeon's technique just because he operates on a criminal."

Rosser Reeves' defense of such practices was reported in Martin Mayer's book, *Madison Avenue U.S.A.* Reeves argued that "The electorate is uninformed and irresponsible before advertising enters. Politicians in their speeches, and partisans writing about the campaign in the press, do not attempt to present the issues of an election in their full complexity. Like the advertising man, they go searching for pat phrases, for slogans."

Such notions forever take us farther from the basic purposes of an election campaign by accepting what is already a shame in American politics and spending millions to enlarge upon it. The true purpose of speech—to develop a fair and desirable competition of ideas—is replaced by an undesirable competition of technicians who work with film to "create" the candidate's image, who deal in schedules to get in the roughest licks too late for an answer, who handle the problems of distribution among radio and television outlets to pick up an advantage over the opposition, who raise the fabulous funds to pay for it all, and who work at a score of other technical jobs which have nothing to do with giving the electorate a fair chance to select the best man.

ANIMAL OR REASON?

Franklyn S. Haiman, Associate Professor of Group Communication at Northwestern University, deploring technique-ridden political concepts, has pointed out that democracy is based on the dignity of individuals who are not governed like lower animals by automatic instincts. A truly democratic choice is a conscious, reasoned choice, but the advertising man's technical prowess is likely to aim at exploiting the animal in man. This, says Dr. Haiman, is a nondemocratic practice. Moreover, the listener in this technique-oriented system must suffer, for in the continual circumventing of reason he is bound to lose contact, or never come to grips with where he really stands.

Thomas R. Nilsen, Associate Professor of Speech at the University of Washington, has written: "... the fewer the distinctly human qualities of reason, self-determination, individuality, which men develop, the better for the political advertising profession. And the worse for democracy, which is based on the assumption that citizens can and will make informed and rational choices.

"By constantly limiting the critical faculties in decision we are limiting the basis upon which it is possible to have a responsible citizenry, and thus we weaken the very foundations of democracy."

All this was most clearly illustrated in the 1964 campaign when one party created a television commercial showing a child picking flowers just before a mushroom cloud blanked out the screen, and the other party made a film that featured a speeding limousine, obviously the President's, with beer cans being tossed from a window. The two films, with their narrations, brought the technique-oriented spoken word to the bottom of the political barrel.

The fact that it can happen under the auspices of our greatest political leaders reveals how far we have wandered from honoring freedom of speech in its true democratic role. This basic freedom is not maintained simply for anyone to say whatever he wants to say. It is established to enhance free and open debate.

"We must insist that free oratory is only the beginning of free speech," says Walter Lippman; "it is not the end but a means to an end. The end is to find the truth. The practical justification of civil liberty is not that self-expression is one of the rights of man. It is that the examination of opinions is one of the necessities of man."

THE PRESIDENT'S SPOKEN POWER

The decline of political debate is all the more serious when considered in light of a momentous change in the American governmental power structure created largely by the modern technological possibilities of spoken language. The Federal executive branch's power has steadily increased over that of the legislative branch. The change has been accelerated as people have become increasingly available to the President's spoken words through radio and television.

In 1933 Franklin D. Roosevelt gave his first Fireside Chat

only eight days after becoming President, and *The New York Times* sensed the coming shift of power. "His use of this new instrument of political discussion," said the *Times*, "is a plain hint to Congress of a resource which the President may employ if it proves necessary to rally support for legislation which he asks and which the lawmakers might be reluctant to give him."

In the first ten months of the Roosevelt Administration, the President, his First Lady and the cabinet gave 144 radio addresses, which brought political protests that FDR was using his office to unfair advantage. But the Presidential advantage was there. As Samuel L. Becker, Associate Professor of Speech at the State University of Iowa, points out: "It was natural that the radio networks were more willing to give time to one President than to ninety-six Senators and 435 Representatives."

FDR, of course, established a precedent not easily dropped. With the coming of television and the first White House broadcast on October 5, 1947, the executive's power through the spoken word was increased all the more. Then former President Eisenhower again expanded the medium's use by moving his press conferences before the television cameras. The innovation eight years later was put to work with even greater effect by the late President Kennedy and his successor President Johnson. Thus in the hands of one man we find the awesome power of modern speech, limited in the numbers of users but almost unlimited in its ability to reach the masses.

THE POWER TO HIDE WORDS

In the same hands is found another executive power of immense strength which also has potential for seriously tampering with that all-important communication between the "gifted and creative leaders" and the people. The President and thousands around him have an unprecedented permit to conduct their affairs in secrecy. This opportunity, which is an enlargement of procedures from World War II, cuts deeply into the public discourse so necessary to a healthy democracy.

The authority for U.S. official secrecy comes from Executive Order 10501 which was signed in 1953 by President Eisenhower but has been adopted with minor changes by succeeding administrations. Security classification as defined by 10501 has been described by a congressional committee as a "catch-all system permitting scores of government agencies and more than a million government employees" to secret all kinds of material and actions. The order is most notorious for its omissions. While the directive threatens severe penalties to those who fail to use secrecy for the abstract purposes of national security, it says nothing about punishing those who misuse secrecy to cover up errors, waste, inefficiency, and the debate of critical issues that may affect the course of history and the destiny of us all. The order offers no effective way for people to appeal the application of secrecy when they feel it is wrong. And 10501, while dealing primarily with the mechanics of *how* to apply secrecy, neglects a more significant question: "*Why* should it be applied?"

The restrictions of this order have been used to prevent public discussion of some of the most momentous issues ever to confront the nation. For example, when the United States, after a long moratorium on atomic testing, decided on a prolonged series of nuclear tests, the action was taken with hardly a word of public debate. *The New York Times*, reluctantly accepting the decision in the name of national security, commented: ". . . Nobody who is not privy to the secret scientific and military considerations that went into the decision can gainsay it." A letter to the *Times* took issue with the editors for their concession to secrecy. Carl Barus, an electrical engineer of Swarthmore, Pennsylvania, wrote: "It is sophistry to suggest that 'secret science and military considerations' determine a unique course of action necessary for our preservation. It amounts to saying that Big Brother knows best."

Officials in the Federal executive branch, working in secret and insulated from public debate and criticism, continually decide grave issues behind doors that jam the essential communication line to the citizens of a democracy. The events that burst forth from these covert discussions are often horrendous. The Bay of Pigs and the U-2 affair are classic examples. A few years after these events, secret councils led our military people in Vietnam from an advisory role to outright acts of war against the North Vietnamese. The change in roles did not receive the public airing a democracy demands, especially before going to war. "Not only was congressional debate avoided," said *The New York Times,* "but there were repeated denials that such a decision had been made. Indeed, the whole effort was to make it appear that nothing had changed in American policy since 1954."

"The Constitution assigns to Congress the right to declare war," wrote Hans J. Morgenthau, Director of the Center for the Study of American Foreign and Military Policy at the University of Chicago. "How can Congress discharge this function if its members and the citizens who have elected them are precluded from discussing the merits of the issues which might lead to war? The Constitution implies that Congress has a choice in the matter of war. How can it make that choice if neither it nor the people it represents have the right to debate the issues? To say that the most momentous issues a nation must face cannot be openly and critically discussed is really tantamount to saying that democratic debate and decision do not apply to the questions of life and death and that, as far as they are concerned, the people have given *carte blanche* to one man."

POTENTIAL FOR DEMAGOGUERY

Fortunately, the weight of their office and the power of their words have sobered our Presidents so that the powerful techniques of modern communication unique to them have more often than not been used with a large degree of responsibility. But around that office, and around our land there is unsettling evidence of speakers and listeners in positions of wealth and power, who use the modern techniques of spoken language without regard to the intellectual integrity that "is one of man's necessities" in a democracy. The warning is clear that America has the human potential for a demagogue, especially if he should arrive in the White House.

Two examples of this potential at work in recent history are found in the movie, "Operation Abolition," and a sound slidefilm, "Communism on the Map." A pair that traveled together, the films were shown to millions of people by sponsorships both surprising and alarming. In Seattle, Washington, for example, the slidefilm was widely exhibited with the help of the Boeing Aircraft Company who made it available to thousands of employees and to the Sand Point Naval Air Station. "Operation Abolition" was sponsored on television by a large national association representing the sales organizations of many large industries. The John Birch Society found the two films excellent for recruiting. In Michigan the state police showed the films to civic, school and professional groups —until Governor John B. Swainson ordered it stopped. And the U.S. Department of Defense bought and placed copies of "Operation Abolition" in its libraries.

"Operation Abolition" was an official production of the House Unamerican Activities Committee which purported to show how the Communists, as part of a master plan to abolish the committee, used California students to disrupt the congressional group's hearings at the San Francisco City Hall. To assemble the movie the committee subpoenaed news films from television films that covered the event. The films were turned over to a commercial filmmaker who then created "Operation Abolition," of which more than 700 prints were sold to sponsors at $100 each.

The main ingredient of "Operation Abolition" is an emotionally charged narration which purports to tell the truth, though it is often fiction or semifiction. It is larded with word-imagery of "disease, contagion, and destruction." The filmed illustrations do not always support the narration, though the unseen speaker proceeds as if the audience were seeing proof of his spoken words. Also, the film editors took considerable license with the true events by juggling the actual time sequences to make them match the narrator's distorted version of what happened.

"The opening day of the hearings, Thursday, May 12," says the narrator, for example, "finds City Hall almost completely surrounded by picketers protesting the committee's appearance." Simultaneously the audience sees a large crowd that was photographed on May 14, when the demonstration was at its height.

Though the narrator talked of student violence and rioting, the motion picture scenes failed to support him, yet his confident voice indicated they did. "The only violence shown in the film," said *The New York Times*, "is that of the police in ejecting many of the protesters from the City Hall. But every one of the sixty-four who were arrested by the police has since been found innocent of wrongdoing by the courts." The demonstrators, pointed out the *Times*, "were almost entirely students who were peacefully, though noisily, protesting what they believed to have been the committee's unfair and unconstitutional conduct and its refusal to admit them to the hearing room packed with friends of the committee."

The reason for this strange film distortion may be found in the movie's opening scenes when a pamphlet is shown briefly as the narrator intones: "This pamphlet is a sample of Communist propaganda. It is published by an organization officially cited as a Communist front. It is, at the instant, being distributed throughout the United States by dedicated, hard-core Communist agents and their dupes. This pamphlet and numerous others like it play a major role as artillery in one phase of the Communist war to destroy our nation— a phase called, by the Communists, 'Operation Abolition.'"

The narrator then says no more about the pamphlet, but reporters found its main substance to be a House of Representatives speech by Congressman James E. Roosevelt. The publisher, hardly a "Communist front," was the Government Printing Office. The publication was the *Congressional Record* in which Congressman Roosevelt was exercising his democratic privilege of calling for abolition of the House committee. The movie's irresponsible rhetoric was the answer.

The narrated strip, "Communism on the Map," is a similar example of irresponsible rhetoric. It implies that Presidents Roosevelt, Truman and Eisenhower did nothing to prevent the spread of communism, indeed, that these three men were unwitting aids to Communist expansion. Support for this contention is frequently *non sequitur* drawn from sources that on the surface seem eminently qualified, but are really irrelevant.

Giovanni Costigan, Professor of History at the University of Washington, analyzed the film strip with its questionable narration as having three possible effects on the uninformed: (1) our NATO allies are useless, (2) our democratic institutions cannot be trusted to resist communism, and (3) we should be prepared to accept the kind of military-controlled government that President Eisenhower warned against in his farewell address. The history professor said the film strip was dominated by fear, suspicion and hatred. After his criticism Professor Costigan received threats upon his life and the name plate was torn from his office door.

OUR RHETORIC OF HATE

The films are only two of a great many examples of the American potential for irresponsible rhetoric. Extremist groups by the mid-1960s were producing it in unbelievable quantity through 7,000 weekly radio and television broadcasts across the nation. The number had increased from a mere 500 in the late 1950s, and the cost had risen to some $10 million a year. One of the broadcasters, the Reverend Carl McIntire, was heard from a single radio station in 1958. A few years later listeners' contributions allowed him to voice his opinions over 617 stations. An example of his rhetoric is the charge that the thirty-one-denomination National Council of Churches is lining up in America's racial conflict "alongside Communist action."

"McIntire," says Idaho's Senator Frank Church, "is only one of several Big Scare purveyors on radio-TV. Their conspiratorial interpretation of each event and their endless debasement of loyal leaders reach the credulous in their huge audience. So the seeds of suspicion are sown, and the harvest is already bitter."

The rhetorically distorted ideas bring Washington senators and representatives a continuing storm of mail reflecting America's channels of hate. One day Senator Thomas Kuchel of California took to the Senate floor to deplore what he calls "fright mail." "Treason!" he said, has become a word used as loosely as the salutation on a letter. "The most heinous crime on the American books. And not always scrawled illiterately on a scrap of paper bag, but often typed meticulously on embossed paper."

Here is an example: "This morning on radio over Mr. Beirpos' program," says a letter from Sacramento, "I heard the most fantastic thing I have ever heard. Water Moccasin —what is this secret fantastic thing going on in the Deep

South. U.N. troops coming to America for some kind of a 'war to invade America.' Mr. Senator, these things are being said over the radio, and he would not say them if they were not true. He said, 'it's a three-point program of the disarmament program.' "

"A distressed schoolteacher," says Senator Church, "writes to warn me that 'our defenses are being destroyed and we are rapidly becoming sitting ducks for our enemies.' If the Communists are successful in seizing control of the country, she continues, 'we will go down together. You, as well as all leaders, will be liquidated. . . . None will be spared unless they are members of the Communist organization.'

"How do you answer such a letter? Its implication—that this sturdy country of ours is about to be taken over—is preposterous. Yet this honest, deeply disturbed woman is being trapped into the belief that treason seethes around her."

SMALL, INTIMATE HATE SESSIONS

The vendors of divisive information recommend that followers speak up in all kinds of gatherings, PTA, Rotary, school boards, churches and on and on. A favorite device is the small, intimate "study" groups for which extremist organizations often supply prerecorded magnetic tapes and phonograph records along with prepared talks to bring the word to students.

In Oklahoma the "Sooner Freedom Forum," is exceptionally strong in the rich, oil city of Bartlesville where an estimated 2,000 people from all walks of life have graduated from the Forum's six-session study groups each of which is limited to fourteen people.

One autumn night in Bartlesville several of these small groups were meeting at one time, in homes of well-to-do citizens and in the Forum's book-lined office. At the office, the group leader, a major oil-company employee, guided by a

House Unamerican Activities Committee document described the political murder and torture that supposedly occurs in Communist China. He explained that Chinese Communists heaped human bodies into large vats where maggots were raised to feed chickens on Communist farms. Women's breasts were being cut off for political reasons, said the Sooner China expert, and prisoners were being nailed to walls. "Now I know this sounds fantastic to us here," said the teacher, "but these are the people who were there." He held up the House Committee pamphlet as evidence. He then turned on a tape-recorded voice, that of a former Franciscan missionary who had more atrocity stories.

The literature of the Sooner Forum directed readers to the Birch Society and other far-right organizations for further study. "Bring anti-Communist programs into organizations to which you belong..." said one piece of material. "Do not let anyone get by with a white-washing statement about communism."

The director of public affairs for one of Bartlesville's largest companies supported the study groups, saying, "I regard it as a sincere effort to keep better informed on communism and the difference between our two systems."

FRIGHTENING ACCEPTANCE

Such blithe acceptance of hate-filled rhetoric by people who would seem to know better is the most frightening part of the irresponsible public communication. Around the nation there are all too many such examples for us to feel comfortable. The following was taken from a *New York Times* dispatch by James Reston who was visiting Mississippi: "... Tom Anderson, one of the leaders of the National Council of the Birch Society, was here in Oxford last night scalding 'Daddybird' Johnson as a 'fraud' and blaming Washington for all the woes and weaknesses of the human race, from Mississippi to Vietnam. Well over 1,000 University of Mississippi students cheered him enthusiastically for one hour and twenty minutes and not one of them challenged either his bad history or his bad manners in the forty-minute question period that followed."

It was a similar, undemanding acceptance of Hitler, more than what he said, that made possible his evil mission. The former Nazi youth leader, Fred L. Casmir, can't help but recall "the ways in which the hateful word 'Communist' was spoken around my home and how my father trusted that in Hitler lay some hope for a country which was torn asunder by internal strife and faced with possible Communist rule."

REVOLT AND AN ACCOMMODATING RHETORIC

But how is it that we find much the same kind of uncritical acceptance of irresponsible rhetoric hurled freely around an affluent America?

First, millions of people are obviously—and in many instances, understandably—dissatisfied with what America offers. Thus they are motivated by an emotionally charged urge to revolt. "It is, clearly, a revolt against the established order by the discontented," says Senator Church, "motivated by a mixture of reasons: a quest for some higher purpose than is satisfied by the commercial standards of our times; a fear of new relationships being generated by the burgeoning growth, urbanization and automation of the country; a resistance to the complexities of modern life, to the bigness of government, to the racial revolution, to a 'cold war' that never ends, to the absence of quick and easy solutions; a frustration over the inability of the United States, in the nuclear age, to swiftly work its will upon the world. These are the conditions of life with which we must cope, but they stir many a rebel to go forth in search of a cause."

Second, this uncritical acceptance is fostered by a mother tongue whose public use is stricken by ill health. We have neither the training nor experience in the spoken communication of public discourse to know right from wrong. Few of us have been taught the oral-aural intellectual skills of separating a valid idea from an emotionally charged verbal effect designed to move people without thought. Meanwhile, everyday experience attunes us to endless spoken words flung our way by the rhetoric of frivolous advertising efforts which are likely to subdue content in favor of ear-catching techniques.

DESTINY STILL IN DANGER

Until the spoken word in our society is put into good order, our mother tongue will remain in ill health and our destiny will continue in danger. The ebb and flow of emotions are likely to determine our course rather than the more sane and intelligent guidance that comes from a good and responsible public speech capable of developing and gaining acceptance for ideas to benefit the majority.

X

The Rhetoric of the Quick Sale

FROM THE EARLY Greeks, to John Quincy Adams, to the present-day professional teachers of speech, traditional rhetoricians have recognized that man's gift of speech has a lofty mission if it is to be wisely used. It is the key communication to the mutual exchange of ideas between men for the purpose of identifying and solving their most essential problems. Speech in this role can serve us in the highest endeavors—government, education, business, science, religion—and in the smallest units of society, such as the continuing discourse that goes with family and friends. All together the daily speech of everyone becomes the fabric of a democracy. As the teacher, Kurt Riezler, has stressed, ". . . democracy lives and has all its strength in the vigor and intensity of mutual response within which the talkers listen and the listeners talk back."

However, if speech is not treated in keeping with this lofty purpose, the quality of the democratic fabric suffers. If, in other words, the spoken word is not ethically committed to important ideas, issues and problems, we lose its inherent quality control of the democratic process.

In America the general neglect of the spoken word has allowed us to lose sight of the high purposes of speech in a healthy democracy. We have forgotten that democracy de-

mands citizens in great number who can contribute daily
through the uses of good and responsible speech. We are neglecting to work at the education of citizens described centuries ago by Marcus Fabius Quintilian as good men who can
speak well.

THE AMERICAN RHETORIC

The results are on display all around. When, more than
ever, we need people to contribute orally to these times,
when the world, and especially our democracy, faces the
greatest issues ever, America does not benefit from a rhetoric
that is ethically committed to matters of importance. In its
neglect, speech has been badly degraded, and we live more by
a "rhetoric of the quick sale," that is not committed to the
interplay of important ideas for the purpose of identifying
and solving the crucial problems of government, politics,
education, religion, and man's treatment of man. Its interest
is consumed by techniques of persuasion that back up the
"hard sell," the "pitch," and the "fast deal." Ideas are not
considered as grist for problem solving, but as products to
sell, like pizza pies or a new gasoline additive. This rhetoric is
memorable only for its vast quantity of mechanically uttered
words unimportant to the good of a democratic society.

Daily, many of us experience the rhetoric of the quick
sale in business meetings, service clubs, civic boards, committees of a thousand kinds and in personal and family conversations where few of the discussants seem to comprehend that
their central role is to arrive at a consensus best for the group
or the larger numbers they represent. Today's conference is
too often viewed, not as an opportunity to weigh ideas, to
deliberate, but as a contest where one or two individuals can
win if they do a better job of selling their points of view.

Concern over this was voiced by the President of the
Brookings Institute, Robert D. Calkins, in a letter to the

Speech Association of America. He asked: "... is any institution trying to develop the skills of public speaking for small conferences, meetings, boards of directors, etc.; or the skills of conference leadership? This form of discussion is the most rapidly growing form in our society and we find it desperately in need of skilled participants. I have seen able advocates and discussants sway boards of directors, conferences, and study groups to accept views and positions quite opposite to their beliefs because no one could reply effectively and restore objective deliberation after a persuasive appeal. If we could develop communication skills to aid informed deliberation and judgment rather than victory in swaying people to an advocate's point of view, American society would be enormously benefitted."

SILENCE ON WHAT'S IMPORTANT

While the speakers who use the rhetoric of the quick sale can be full of fury when profits are at stake, or when matters at hand are no more weighty than a cake sale or the Little League, they often go silent when confronted by the great ideas and problems of our time. These are often the controversial ideas, and controversy is seldom considered good for sales. Thus our most prevalent rhetoric—and it may be just as well—is narrowly involved with the business at hand.

Its restricted, uncourageous quality is what U.S. Supreme Court Justice, William O. Douglas, deplored when he gave the first annual lecture for the Earl Warren Institute on Ethics and Human Relations in Los Angeles. Conformity, he said, has smothered America's traditional debate and discussion. "Big business, big government, big unions—each has helped erase some of the qualities of individuality from Americans," concludes Justice Douglas. "As the individual has become more and more submerged, his voice is more indistinct."

THE EXEMPLARY ARE FEW

Indeed, this description fits so well that one is hard put to point out examples of people in large numbers who are ethically committed to solving today's great human problems with man's most persuasively powerful tool, the spoken word. There are, of course, exceptions and, fortunately for us, many of them are devoting time and carrying great burdens in education, religion, government and political organizations. No better example has been on the national scene for a longer time than Norman Thomas, the man who ran so often as the Socialist candidate for the Presidency. For years he has spoken to America with courage and conviction about its most crucial issues. But there are far too few men like Norman Thomas, who truly fits that ancient description of the good man skilled in speaking.

A singularly great group example of Americans ethically committed to human value is that of the Negro as he struggles for civil rights, particularly in the South. His movement has been fueled very much by the responsible use of the spoken word, which in turn has often been uplifted to great oratorical heights by the Negro's total commitment to his cause. Civil rights persuasion, unable to depend upon the printed word in the press and other media, has come largely from Negro speakers talking to their people in their churches. These oratorical efforts have been lighted with ideas which the speakers have stood by at all costs short of committing violence. At the same time the Negro has given us a memorable example of speech used with a unique sense of ethics, for he has shown us how rhetorical power well used can stir an entire people to resist restrictive and often hateful measures without violence, though violence has often come their way.

The Negro's rhetorical commitment is in sharp contrast

to what most of us speak for or remain silent about. It stands clearly against the fact that great numbers of Americans equate the word "controversy" with something subversive, and that thousands see no difference between valid dissent and dissension. While the Negro speaks out, droves of well-dressed, extensively educated men won't express the meekest political opinion for fear of hurting business. Entire communities avoid important issues, like prayer in the schools, for fear of disturbing what they consider social equilibrium. If something controversial does come up for discussion, a few whispered criticisms can often stop the movement. In towns where churches are filled on Sunday morning, the subject of religion remains undiscussed for the week's remaining six-and-a-half days; everyone understands how it can mess up commercial ventures. In most communities only a handful of qualified individuals can be found to participate in political jobs, and on the boards, committees and panels that are settling some of our most crucial affairs. Getting too mixed up in things is bad for business. The weather is the safest subject to take up publicly, so wind, rain, snow and temperature provide the issues on which most Americans dare commit themselves. Everyone discusses the weather.

WHERE THE PATTERNS ARE SET

The society in which this form of rhetoric can thrive was described as early as 1951 by Robert S. Lynd, author of the classic study of an American community, entitled "Middletown." "The culminating 'racket' quality of private power in American life defeats all efforts to strengthen the democratic process," said Lynd. "Not only are private interests increasingly manipulating public opinion and diverting attention from democratically important issues ... but ... all of us are being turned psychologically against such rationalizing steps as national economic planning by the contagious preoccupation with 'getting a break,' cutting in on a racket of our own. . . ."

The rhetoric fostered by such a society, low in ethics and commitment, has many social and psychological forces to shape it, but one stands out clearly above the rest. At the leadership levels of American life we find models for the lack of ethical commitment, so that much of what happens at life's less influential levels seems to seep down from the top. How can we expect a rhetoric of ethical commitment from large areas of our population when bosses, leaders, even educators engage in just the opposite—indeed, when they often pay handsome sums for development and promotion of a rhetoric interested only in the gains at hand, ethics be damned?

For this form of oral communication at topside there are many examples, but one that tells the story well is the widespread acceptance of ghost writers by leaders of business, government, education and religion. Ghost writers, responsible for billions of spoken words in America, certainly are not individuals committed to important ideas. Most frequently their products are insipid, dull talks framed with oversimplified "canned ideas" selected mainly to please the man who pays the ghost. The manufactured orations seldom provide us with examples of speech from men who have a burning desire to help their fellow men solve their most trying problems. If the speeches have any teeth at all, the bite usually involves a self-serving cause aimed at benefiting the speaker more than anyone else.

A SHOESHINE AND A SPEECH

Thus, the ideational side of speech has been delegated to the baggage handling department. When asked not long ago if he used a ghost writer, a businessman answered: "Of course; I don't shine my own shoes, do I?"

The magazine *Management Review* once carried advice on how to use a speech writer. A good reason for hiring one, said the article, is that he will have time to think and write while an important executive has no such time. To the ghost, continues the publication, this kind of thinking and writing is a major responsibility, while the executive must treat it as "something he does in his spare moments in between important chores." "A person discharging a major responsibility," continues the article, "usually does a better job than one who performs the task as a time-consuming sidelight to more important (and perhaps more profitable) duties."

With that attitude the purchasers of prepared speeches often receive material whose ideas never rise above the spit-and-polish level. Here, for some revealing examples, are the thoughts of a few busy ghosts, as quoted in the *Saturday Review:*

"This is hack work. The tragedy of it is that we might really be able to make a contribution in helping the business community communicate its views if only the businessmen would take us seriously. Unfortunately, most businessmen just aren't interested in ideas. They think that a speech, like an income tax form, is something you pay someone to prepare."

"I rarely ever see the man for whom I'm writing. I usually just put together some 'canned' ideas that I think will please the old boy."

"I regard my speeches as pure fiction. And where can you get better pay for fiction these days?"

From the mouths of ghosted speakers, who have circumvented thoughtful preparation, often come words which clearly reveal that connections have never been established between the orators' vocal chords and brains. One year at its convention, the Speech Association of America held a session whose theme was "Speech in Government." One of the speakers from Washington listened to the first few talks and then rose and read about three minutes of his prepared speech before a fact that had immediately struck the audience jolted his mind: his speech was word-for-word the same ghostwritten piece of work mouthed by the first speaker.

The United States Government is unquestionably the work site for more ghost writers than any other body in the world, but the practice is frowned upon in many other governments. In these anti-ghost societies, a speaker is expected to be the individual who thought up or thought about what he says. For example, in the British House of Commons the Conservative Prime Minister Sir Alec Douglas-Home was berated by indignant members of the Labour Party for having used a *Newsweek* magazine writer to iron out some spoken words. The Prime Minister admitted to the charge but "solemnly declared that no speech writers are employed by any of Her Majesty's official agencies 'as such.' " But no Washington official needs answer this kind of charge, for Federal ghost writers—usually called "information specialists"—are firmly fixed and widely accepted.

A Washington magazine reporter, Don Oberdorfer, poses a serious facet of the problem thusly: "A ... realistic danger is that the mounting volume of ghostwritten verbiage by people with nothing much to say will deaden our public discourse, producing something akin to oratorical inflation. Ghostwritten pronouncements can be lethal only if they bore us all to death."

THE ETHICS OF WHO'S TALKING

While ghosted rhetoric is hardly a committed rhetoric, neither is it an ethical form of communication. This is compounded by the fact that ethical considerations are more critical with the spoken word than the written, for in the oral situation one encounters factors that enlarge upon all the possibilities for dishonesty.

A speaker's very presence strongly implies that what he has to say is his, from the words, the tone of voice, the gestures and all the other verbal and nonverbal factors. People travel great distances, wait in lines, pay money and sit in crowded, stuffy rooms to hear what this or that individual has to say. Even if they read his words, to get the same material from the source has special meaning and value, for over the ages it has been deeply impressed upon us that the spoken word in all of its nonverbal trimmings offers the best chance for assessing ideas and the person uttering them.

A ghost writer behind the scenes naturally tampers with this process so important to the assessment of speakers by listeners. By providing or styling the material that makes and structures spoken ideas the ghost affects both the verbal and nonverbal attributes of the spoken word. For instance, the speaker given to making rash statements may no longer do so when he is ghosted, yet his natural rashness may by itself have more to communicate than anything he might say. In another instance the stumbling and fumbling for words by a talker may say something to the listener that is missing when phrases have been carefully chosen and polished by a ghost writer.

A rhetorical study of the 1946 to 1950 speeches of the industrialist Benjamin Fairless reveals that in the first three of these years he used poor language, but suddenly in April 1950, it was dramatically improved. Coincidentally, in the same month Fairless' public-relations department acquired a new speech writer, Phelps Adams. If the startling change in the industrialist's speeches came through Adams' pen, how can it be said that his listeners were any longer hearing the true Benjamin Fairless? A relevant question would ask where Adams stopped and Fairless began in this voice that led a great corporation.

A DOUBLE STANDARD

Why can so many people accept a speech ghost writer without concern for ethics? The answer brings us back to the general attitude that says speech is unimportant, that it is something which falls into the category of janitor services. Who wastes time thinking about the ethics of window washing, shining the brass—or polishing words? Not those who can afford ghost writers.

When speech is so degraded, a double standard is applied to ghostwriting, i.e., we are distressed by the absence of ethics in many areas of life while financially supporting an unethical practice in the field of speech. This was demonstrated in New York City when a newspaper reporter posed as a ghost writer and discovered how certain agencies sell their services to students and scholars to ghost write term papers and theses for advanced academic degrees. One of the most startling cases was that of a Southwestern university professor who paid $1,250 for a ghosted doctoral dissertation. While the law questioned the legality of the business, a state's attorney observed that besides writing scholarly papers, the agencies had a "legitimate" trade ghosting speeches. When a Minneapolis paper tried to clarify the ethics involved the editor emphasized that "College degrees are taken to represent honest, independent academic ability and achievement." This brought a comment from Ernest G. Bormann, a speech professor at the University of Minnesota, who said: "Apparently speeches by businessmen, governors and the President of the United States are not to be taken as representative of honest, independent ability and achievement."

A standard defense for using a ghost says that the spoken ideas can be the speaker's even though the words are not his. The speaker in a quick meeting or by letter tosses out the thoughts he wishes to convey and the ghost takes it from there, filling out the speech framework. His employer plays architect while he plays carpenter.

But this procedure in itself raises the question of ethics because the true and full nature of an idea is not likely to become evident or at all useful until the owner himself has taken the pains to put it into words. Thus the ethical question becomes more or less acute according to the speaker's degree of involvement in the preparation of what he has to say. If he simply starts the process and allows it to be finished by an individual who remains behind the scenes, then a question of honesty is involved. The more the speaker involves himself in the details of his talk, the less dishonest he is with the listeners. In other words, the language a man uses is so closely interwoven with his ideas that he can't ethically duck the job of working it out.

This has been stressed by Professor Borman at the University of Minnesota when he said "... there is a long and honorable tradition that style is one of the most important elements of rhetoric. Language is not a trivial part of speech-making; deception is involved in changing a man's characteristic mode of expression."

Obviously few of us have taken the time or been given the educational motivation to think about the basic relationships between ethics and what we say and how we say it. A blatant example of our ignorance and indifference to the problem is found in the *Management Review* advice on the use of a ghost writer. Under the heading, *Ability to accept praise for the other man's work,* a strange and wobbily ethical comment reads: "Are you willing to accept full credit for your ghosted speech? This means not only standing up to criticism but also accepting praise when it is due. It takes real force of character to act in all respects as though the speech you just gave is yours alone; the temptation is great to give credit to your ghost when the speech is well received, or to disclaim responsibility when something backfires. How do you behave when a good friend praises the talk you have just given? Do you thank him with a normal degree of modesty, or do you become embarrassed—and show it? What do you do when an important person—perhaps a client—calls you to let you know how angry or disappointed he is in what you had to say? Do you say that you are sorry, but that is what you think —or do you try to pass it off as just 'one of those things a ghost prepared for me?'

"It does more harm than good to deliver a speech that you're going to disclaim at the first opportunity. If you aren't prepared to stand behind what you say, it's pointless to go to the trouble of speaking at all."

GHOST OR COLLABORATOR?

Granted that some extremely busy people are pressed into a great many routine speeches—the President of the United States being the notable example—and of course they need assistance. Some of the greatest orators of recent history were helped by speech writers. However, a look at the relationships between these speakers and writers often reveals that the latter served more as collaborators than as outright ghosts. Franklin Delano Roosevelt made liberal use of speech writers, but it is well known that the late President spent a great deal of time reworking the major efforts of the writers who were closest to him.

Of all the recent Presidential candidates few have been admired by the speech profession more than the late Adlai Stevenson whose speeches are considered modern classics though he lost both elections in which he ran. "To Stevenson," says Russel Windes, Jr., Assistant Professor of Public Address at Northwestern University, "there is something deceptive about this process [ghostwriting]. For the same reason, he dislikes the makeup, the teleprompters and any of the gadgetry and device of showmanship and political razzle-dazzle that tends to color a candidate. He feels that these artifices obscure from the people the one thing they must know —the real thoughts, personality and character of the man they are asked to vote for."

In his last Presidential campaign Stevenson had a group of well-known writers to help him with the 250-speech burden in the eight weeks before election. They wrote draft after draft of each speech but Stevenson kept changing the manuscript even as he walked to the platform. In his last minute rewrites on fifteen speeches the candidate made 976 changes, averaging sixty-five per speech. In three of the speeches he made 125 changes on each talk. He also made impromptu alterations as he talked. In one forty-five-minute speech Stevenson made 174 alterations while he spoke.

EVERYBODY WANTS A SPEAKER

Of course, a Presidential candidate is forced to use ghost writers because he has to speak so much—indeed, too much— and in many other instances, this is a nub of the ghostwriting problem in general. Speech is cheap in America. Anyone of the slightest eminence, qualified or not, is some time asked to speak—and all too often the unqualified individual who really has nothing to say accepts. The demand for speakers by all sorts of organizations far exceeds the supply of persons trained or experienced at preparing and giving a speech.

At the same time we suffer an oversupply of poor listeners who do not have the critical sense to demand good speech ethically committed to issues of importance. These facts of supply and demand open the door for thousands of speeches lacking both commitment and the ethics of self-preparation. Thousands of questionable orators enter the open door.

The filling of speech engagements has become big business in industry, and the effort swells the already swollen supply of ghosted speakers talking on narrow, unimportant themes. Public-relations departments have recognized that the thousands of possible speaking engagements before millions of uncritical listeners offer added opportunities to pump out company messages to the public. The result has been the growth of company speakers bureaus through which employees, after a short course in the techniques of speaking, go forth to recite mimeographed addresses for America's speech-hungry organizations.

TELLING THE DRUG STORY

A primary example is the pharmaceutical industry which makes the nation's prescription drugs. Seven major companies of this industry, known as the "ethical" drug trade where consumer advertising is frowned upon, had 1,322 trained employee-speakers according to one survey. The speakers, located all over the country were working with sixteen different prepared speeches which had been presented 7,842 times to 320,112 people. Nearly half (48 per cent) of this large listening audience were service-club members.

The most active of the seven speakers bureaus had trained 664 speakers of whom 445 were active. This one bureau, using five different prepared speeches, accounted for more than half the total presentations of all the bureaus. About eighteen months after the survey the number of speakers had increased to over 700 and about 2,500 speaking engagements had been added to the total.

This ethical drug house has taken its speech mission seriously enough to provide full-time employment for two former speech professors and a staff. They travel the country giving short intensive speech courses to the firm's "detail" men (who introduce and sell ethical drugs to doctors and pharmacies). The course concentrates upon the ability to read orally. In the firm's home office the speakers bureau has an elaborate, closed-circuit television studio where speakers can practice and then watch themselves in action on a video-tape system.

Activity in the bureau is strictly voluntary and the management emphasizes that it is unrelated to promotions. But a speaking job well done is recognized with rewards that include cash, bonds, jewelry, silverware and other merchandise or certificates for it. Speakers are also publicized and praised at least indirectly in the bureau publications.

When a bureau speaker goes to a meeting he arrives before his audience with a speech printed in large, widely spaced type that is easily followed. This script, written at company headquarters, has numerous instructions, including stage directions. For instance, on the left margin vertical lines identify paragraphs that the company speaker may edit out if time runs short.

The speaker also comes with a number of props for which his manuscript sometimes carries annotated instructions to help him employ the paraphernalia at the right moment. Certain gestures and emphatic pauses are also prompted by notes in the script. Whenever an instruction calls for the speaker to lift his eyes from the printed speech, a large asterisk appears just before the next sentence to help return his vision to the right spot for continuous, uninterrupted reading.

The manuscript even helps the speaker acquire a certain natural effect by *ad libbing*. A small asterisk occasionally appears in the text, leading the speaker to the bottom of the page where he finds his company-prepared *ad lib* in print.

THE KEFAUVER SIDE

The bureau's management readily admits that the investigations of the late Senator Estes Kefauver had a lot to do with the extensive speaking effort. Anyone who followed the

Senator's work knows there is more than the industry side to the modern story of ethical drugs, but in the American rhetorical climate it would of course be naive to expect prescription-drug-industry speakers, with their training and annotated scripts, to apprise service clubs and other organizations of all that came out of the Kefauver investigations. This congressional material concerning drug prices, profits and research made the industry worry over its "image."

This concern was revealed by a company-financed opinion survey on a talk that its speakers use extensively. The testing of how the prepared speech affected eight different audiences indicated the speech worked in favor of the industry. It showed that the talk "strengthens the industry's image," "reduces criticism of the industry's prices," "contributes to an improved understanding of profits," and "increases opposition to government price control of prescription drugs."

The corporate craving to line up public opinion in favor of management's point of view is often evident in topics offered by many of the various speakers bureaus. A major Detroit auto manufacturer, for instance, has a large number of speakers fulfilling engagements with standard prepared company speeches. The topics include talks on automation, car styling and guided missiles, which are subjects in which the firm certainly has vested interests measured in millions.

THERE ARE POSSIBILITIES, BUT. . . .

An industrial speakers bureau operated for the public's interest holds many possibilities for public education. Moreover, a speakers bureau puts the company's personnel on a platform before the public where they are open to questions and criticism that otherwise they might not hear. And regardless of how the speaker carries out his assignment, the very fact that he is standing on his own feet talking to people who are out of his general field of interest can hardly help but have some positive results.

On the other hand these speakers bureaus, each with their prepared talks so closely tied to techniques and so concerned with the narrow business at hand, can hardly be considered a commendable reflection on America's speaking and listening habits.

First, consider the speaker who allows himself—even though his involvement is said to be completely voluntary— to serve as the mouthpiece for the notions that his employer, usually a corporate organization, wants to promote in behalf of that abstract thing called "image." These industrial orators can hardly be described as individuals ethically committed to the great issues of our time.

Moreover, it is hard to believe that they are even ethically committed to the very ideas that they are promoting. An individual with something of burning importance on his mind does not need the enticement of rewards of money or merchandise or personal publicity to say it. If he *has* to speak about something, no mimeographed speech with instructions for gesture and verbal expression will contain him.

Perhaps the most serious effect of these tightly controlled speech efforts is that they do not uplift the spoken word in a time when it badly needs bolstering. Their finely filtered points of view certainly increase by many fold the uncommitted oral presentations which seldom stir ideas and thoughts toward the solution of man's most important problems.

ELECTRONIC NONCOMMITMENT

Yet in the entire panorama of American speech, the speakers bureaus are but one element in the disregard for ethical commitment. A greater force is found in most of our homes where the average American spends more than a quarter of his waking hours turned to radio and television.

The performing heroes of these miraculous inventions are seldom, if ever, men committed to important ideas. It would seem that the job description for certain radio or television stars calls for a fantastic ability to talk for long periods without saying anything consequential. Hour upon hour of broadcasted words, mixed with recorded music, old movies, cartoons and millions of commercials, build up to Himalayas of trivia. Indeed, it takes a peculiar skill for a man to talk almost steadily through a microphone from 6:00 to 9:00 A.M. without saying anything more pointed than to question the cliché that all men should despise their mothers-in-law.

This general neglect of anything important was documented in a study conducted from Ohio State University by Joseph M. Ripley, Jr., who contacted all the U.S. radio and television stations that had been on the air a year or more. From the answers the Ohio investigator found the stations seriously omitting opinions and controversial issues. An abstract of the study says:

"While the majority of broadcasters who returned questionnaires had made their facilities available to holders of opinions on controversial issues, a significant proportion of the respondents did not make time available; a few even reported having policies against making time available for this purpose. Generally speaking, the broadcasters did not devote a great deal of time to discussions of controversial issues. Furthermore, many of the formats used by those who made some time available did not provide adequately for confrontation, for representation of all pertinent points of view, or for the opportunity to present an opinion fully.

"While a majority of the broadcasters who replied had policies that assured their audiences of fair treatment of both sides, more than half the stations were not fulfilling their obligations in practice. Hence, the broadcasters generally were not operating in the fullest interest of a democratic society in this area of programming."

BREEDING "NO-THINKS"

How can this happen in a democracy whose founders and builders were so committed to the discussion of issues from every point of view? One reason is that we have audiences that allow and relish it, great masses of listeners who have neither the kind of education nor the experience it requires to ascertain what is and what isn't "in the fullest interest of a democratic society."

Justice William O. Douglas has said that commercial television and radio—along with big business, big government and big unions—"breed noncontroversial men and women. . . .

"There has been such a deadening effect of radio and TV on the American mind," he adds, "that we may have reached a point where men and women who will sponsor unorthodox points of view must be subsidized by foundations. . . ."

What the Justice says, of course, is not only of recent concern. The following, for instance, is a similar statement made as a comment on the Army-McCarthy Hearings by Ben Park, Network Program Manager of NBC's Central Division: "Frank and opinionated discussion of all issues, without regard for the consequences of conclusions logically arrived at, is absolutely necessary to the functioning of the open society. Nevertheless, we have seen fit, in the name of national survival, to curtail a considerable amount of the intellectual expression once enjoyed in the United States. And the citizenry has accepted this condition. The mass-communication media have softened them up, it seems to me, by stating only superficially the end results, and by over simplifying the underlying causes, pressures and arguments. And the media has done this because they supposed, with some justification, that they were giving the public what it wanted."

Such complaints withstanding, there listlessly sits the

great audience. Most nights they are in the living rooms thoughtlessly absorbing frivolities with TV dinners and six-packs of beer. On nights out or at luncheons the same audience populates thousands of meetings sponsored by organizations with the flimsiest excuses for forming—as witness the California group called TOPS (Take Off Pounds Successfully). Week after week the audience eats bland food and suffers a speaker, whose opening remarks in contest with the clearing of dishes from the tables, signal the time to daydream of other things. When listening does occur, it follows the same aural habits exhibited in front of radio and TV. The speaker's words and techniques are digested along with the poor food, without question.

HOW DO YOU KNOW?

The rhetoric of the quick sale in America thrives on this audience whose poor listeners are as much responsible for our uncommitted rhetoric as the talkers. Until we do something to change this audience for the better, this rhetoric is likely to continue on the low road that misses most of the important issues we should be talking about. But the change won't come about as long as most members of the vast American audience come from public schools where the subject of critical listening never comes up, and where students do not encounter the rhetorical principles which could help one recognize when a speaker's glib techniques should be placed in the same category as cheating in a test, on the baseball field or in a card game.

The rhetoric of the quick sale will continue to inundate any rhetoric ethically committed to what is important in our time until the schools take steps to educate people who can think well orally and aurally through the spoken word and understand that basic honesty is best served when they can rightfully and skillfully say: "This is what I believe and here is why."

XI

The Citizen Moderator

THE RYAN BROTHERS, Tom and Jerry, are undoubtedly the best known potato farmers in the Red River Valley. The twin brothers own farms totaling some 5,000 acres which annually produce about 300,000 bushels of potatoes. In East Grand Forks, Minnesota, they run a plant which processes potatoes for their own farms and others in the area. In a year the Ryans handle some two million bushels.

One August not long ago I spent a day with Tom and Jerry Ryan. The business hours began in the office of their East Grand Forks plant where the two brothers and several assistants were seated around a large desk with several telephones. The group spent most of the morning in what seemed like an unending conference with each other and dozens of potato farmers, marketers and government officials all over the Red River Valley, and even across the nation. The men took orders, asked questions, quoted prices and discussed problems related to the growing and selling of potatoes.

At noon the Ryan Brothers drove across the Red River to a Grand Forks, North Dakota, restaurant where they were joined by three scientists, one from the U.S. Department of Agriculture and two from the University of North Dakota. Seated at a large round table the group ate a hearty meal and discussed "preharvest methods." The main question was whether it is best, before digging potatoes, to kill the vines with chemicals or with a machine that beats them into fine pieces which are then spread over the fields. While the Ryan brothers were interested in what the scientists had to say, it was obvious that the reverse was also very much the case.

That afternoon the five men drove around the Ryan farms talking as they went. Frequently they parked, left their automobiles and carried on their discussion in the fields while looking over the potato crop. Back in East Grand Forks about five o'clock the Ryan Brothers made a number of last-minute telephone calls before rejoining the visiting scientists in another restaurant where the talk continued into the evening.

Between eight that morning and nine that night the Ryan Brothers were engaged in almost endless communication and, except for a minor percentage, it was all in spoken words. Much of it was naturally routine in nature, but a large part of the discussion was undoubtedly influential to agriculture in the Red River Valley, as well as to potato-growing in general. It was obvious that the Ryans serve as a two-way communication link between dozens of farmers on the one hand and marketers and the government on the other hand.

UNSUNG LEADERS

In this role, either of the two brothers fits the description of a type of American leader who has received a lot of attention over the past few decades from social scientists, mass-communication researchers and others engaged in the study of human conduct. This informally chosen, publicly unheralded leader, of whom there are tens of thousands, comes under various labels, like "opinion leader," "influential," "community leader" or, most often, "group leader."

One important study described this role thusly: "What we shall call opinion leadership, if we may call it leadership at all, is leadership at its simplest; it is casually exercised, sometimes unwitting and unbeknown, within the smallest grouping of friends, family members and neighbors. It is not leadership on the high level of a Churchill, nor of a local politico, nor even of a local social elite. It is at quite the opposite extreme: it is the almost invisible, certainly inconspicuous, form of leadership at the person-to-person level of ordinary, intimate, informal, everyday contact."

This leader is one of society's key communicators, one who relies chiefly on the spoken word. His education as an oral communicator should be of great concern in our schools, for his skill in using and guiding the use of spoken language has a direct bearing on the health of public discussion which is so integral a part of a democracy. This is especially true because the group leader is often the communicative link that holds the key to development and maintenance of what Andrew Thomas Weaver of the University of Wisconsin described as "working understandings between the gifted and creative leaders on the one hand, and the great body of ordinary citizens on the other hand." How well, or how poorly this concept works in our behalf is directly related to the educational cultivation and improvement of the spoken word —not only for those who would be leaders, but also for the vast majority of citizens who assume the role of followers.

UNNOTICED GROUPS

To comprehend the need described here, one should first start by seeing how these followers (really the population at large) are grouped and then how the groups work through individuals who, by way of some perfectly natural tendencies, become their leaders. All this may be explained by briefly reviewing the findings of social scientists and other researchers over many years. Let's start with the phenomenon called the "rediscovery of the primary group."

In a number of instances scientists setting forth to study

human beings in certain environments, such as in industry or the armed services, pretty much limited their research to the environments and the individuals within it, but they soon found that a third element played an important part in determining how people act under certain conditions. This third element was, in a sense, a case of the scientists having to rediscover something they already knew, i.e., that people have a natural tendency to group together for different causes which they then can follow as "one of the gang," or "part of a clique." But in the studies of environmental effects on people, scientists quite naturally overlooked this tendency as being an important factor until, in a number of instances, they were forced to recognize it. This recognition has been called in sociology the "rediscovery of the primary group."

One of the earlier instances occurred in the now famous industrial study of Western Electric's Hawthorne plant. The researchers studied the effects on workers of such things as wages, working hours, illumination and rest periods (in other words, environment). For investigative purposes they worked with a special test group of employees whose environment could be controlled somewhat. But regardless of what the controls did, whether they were good or bad for the employees, productivity rose steadily as though working conditions made no difference. The researchers were naturally puzzled until remarks from members of the test group revealed the answer. They said they liked being part of the study itself and that the satisfactions of being in this special group were so strong that they outweighed adverse environmental changes such as lower wages, poor illumination, or reduction of rest periods. Thus the scientists eventually recognized that the experiment itself had formed a "primary" group which affected the results they were trying to discover.

The investigators then turned their attention to the plant as a whole and found that workers quite naturally and informally banded together in groups that in themselves played a leading role in individual productivity. But this natural grouping didn't always work to increase productivity; in some cases it was decreased.

The Hawthorne study is a classic case of scientists "rediscovering the primary group." The same thing happened again in other important sociological studies, such as an extensive one made of the American soldier during World War II. Also scientists studying community life in America had the experience of "rediscovering the primary group" in the social structure of towns and cities.

This becomes important to our consideration of the spoken word because the phenomenon of rediscovery was also encountered by scientists studying mass communication in America. It became an important element in the study of human persuasion and information flow and it helped scientists more clearly picture how the primary group forms and functions under the kind of leader that prompts this chapter's discussion. This whole pattern of social groups and leaders, as we shall see, is very much a function of the spoken word and how it is used.

THE VOTER'S HABITS

Some of the earliest mass-communication studies involving "rediscovery of the primary group" were directed at how our voting habits are formed by the mass media. Investigators started with a natural assumption that mass media in an election campaign could be practically considered on a one-to-one basis; for example, to study the political effect of a radio speech the researcher would simply need to look at typical listeners and assess the results produced with them by the broadcast.

It didn't turn out to be that simple because once more the scientists found that the effect of mass media upon people is not an unbroken, direct line from broadcaster to typical listeners. Again the difference was made by the way people naturally group themselves so that the group structure itself becomes a factor in persuasion and information flow. Instead of a direct line from mass media to people, it was found that a two-step flow of persuasion and information was more closely the true case.

An understanding of this two-step flow gives us an insight into the important roles often played by a comparatively few, informally chosen leaders who live and work among us. In an election campaign, the scientists found, voters are not as affected by the political words they read and hear as they are by what is said by fellow members of their "primary group." This group may consist of an individual's family, his neighbors, his fellow workers or associates in a club or church. While the typical individual may listen carefully to campaign speeches, or read editorials and magazine articles that attempt to persuade him, he is likely to reserve judgment until he gets the opinion of his peers on the subject. But he pays more attention to some peers than others, and here we find how the factor of leadership enters the communication picture.

In society's naturally formed groups certain individuals sort of float to the top to become the leaders of opinion for the followers who remain below. Those who rise are not necessarily "born" leaders, and while they are at the top of one interest group, perhaps concerned with public affairs, the same people may be followers in another group with a different concern. But in their leadership positions, wherever they are, these individuals seem to exhibit some fairly understandable traits. For instance, they are better informed on the prime subject interests of their groups. If it is public affairs a group leader is likely to be comparatively well versed in politics and he is pretty certain to develop and promote strong opinions.

These opinion leaders, therefore, have an important modulating effect upon our mass media. While their followers may be widely exposed to mass-communication media, such as radio, television and the press, its interpretation is flavored by the leader's thinking. Therefore, one can say, for all intents and purposes, that the products of mass communication come first to him and are then interpreted by him for his followers.

In the famous study of voting habits conducted in Erie County, Ohio, during the 1940 Presidential election campaign, researchers found among 3,000 subjects that while people listened to and read about the Roosevelt-Willkie campaign on the radio and through the press, these media had little direct effect on many voters. Where voters changed their minds about the candidates during the campaign, they frequently said they were prompted to do so while talking to other people. Indeed, the mind changers, who were least interested of all in the campaign, exhibited the most susceptibility to the talk of their peers, as well as the most sheeplike traits of all the followers. This same kind of personal influence, we might note, was also responsible for making voters of some three-fourths of the people who early in the campaign were so obviously disinterested that they did not intend to vote at all.

POTENT PERSUASION

The research scientists in this study recognized that personal influence, usually wielded by group leaders, who in turn got much of their information more directly from the mass media, was a most potent form of persuasion in our society. The investigators saw several reasons why it was so. Note, as the reasons are explained below, how much they are a function of the spoken word.

1. The persuasion exerted through face-to-face, personal contact has a powerful advantage of seeming nonpurposive. The discussions in which such persuasion occurs are usually

begun for routine reasons having nothing to do with the subject of the persuasive discourse that sooner or later enters the conversation. Thus the listener is, in a sense, caught unprepared and has his mind changed while hardly aware of it. Also such discourse carries with it the titillating thought that in the nonpurposive discussion the listener is privy to a general undercurrent of public opinion and, to follow it, will take him along with the right, public supported course of action.

2. The personal persuasion so often exerted by group leaders has the advantage of great flexibility which is impossible for the mass media to incorporate. By the leader's intimate moment-by-moment chance to be guided by verbal and nonverbal feedback from his listener, he is able to shift the immediate course of his argument to bolster his cause, or to do whatever is necessary to work most effectively upon the person he is persuading. The leaders who rise above their group of followers are likely to be especially good at such face-to-face influence.

3. The personal persuader has another advantage of enticement by being able to offer immediate rewards for compliance to what he desires. For agreement from his listeners he can give a smile, a pat on the back or a commendation saying that their action is to everyone's benefit. Such rewards are more valuable to some people than cash prizes, for all through life we seek and learn to relish acceptance, from our parents, teachers, employers and, in this instance, from those who take the reins of leadership in society's informal groupings. The effective leader can use these simple rewards as bait to encourage compliance. The mass media that he may be reflecting can hardly offer the same, on-the-spot return.

4. People, in general, trust an intimate source of information more than they do the overt and distant mass media. The most trust is offered the words of people, especially the

leader types, of the same social status. These casually familiar personal persuaders do not seem to have an ax to grind as do candidates, commentators and others appearing or writing through the mass media.

5. The persuasion of personal influence often meets success with comparative ease, because many of its less informed, uncommitted listeners change their minds without conviction. People responding to this kind of face-to-face influence often agree they have changed their minds but can't say why —as was the case of 25 per cent of the people who shifted from one candidate to the other in the 1940 voting study. In other words an opinion shift results from what is apparently the simple, no-think inclination to do what the rest of the gang is doing despite the meaning. A group leader, of course, is in an advantageous position for stimulating this reaction.

Though not emphasized in the voting study, another persuasive tool is uniquely available to a group leader. He has at his disposal the powerful medium of group discussion while the mass media is pretty much limited to direct, one-way persuasive communication. It has been found that group discussion is likely to be more effective for bringing people around to a decision than spoken persuasion coming from a single person. Such discussions, though most informal, occur continually within the social groups in which all of us participate and the group leaders have a great deal to do with how decisions shall go, for they can guide the discourse that helps followers make up their minds. Discussion also offers some of the group feelings so important to their kind of persuasion. A discussion leading to a decision gives each member a chance to see that he is not "going it alone" but is part of the crowd moving toward something that everyone approves. This, of course, is much less true as an individual sits alone in his living room reading a paper or listening to the one-way messages of radio or television.

THE EVIDENCE BUILDS

The crucial role and the strength of personal influence has been confirmed in other studies following the 1940 one on voting. After World War II an extensive investigation was made in Decatur, Illinois, to begin "mapping the flow of influence concerning several everyday matters in a middle-sized American city." The research was designed "to locate and learn something about these everyday influentials" who serve in face-to-face communication with informal groups and "guide" opinion rather than make it.

The Decatur study revealed that personal influence is much more extensive than one might think. It is, for instance, a deciding factor in the way people buy consumer goods, the selection of movies, and the trends in fashion, reading and record listening. The study's findings portray our society as being a complex patchwork of informal, unlabeled groups interwoven with one another and with a lot of overlap between them. The leaders for these groups, as indicated earlier, rise above their followers for different reasons depending on what each group is all about. An individual is not likely to be a group leader in many different areas of concern (though it is entirely possible); each leader is likely to ascend to his position for reasons that arise from his group's special interest.

UNDERLYING CIRCUITS EVERYWHERE

The Decatur study, and the others in the social sciences, provide impressive evidence that despite the great inventions of the mass media a large part of the nation's most decisive communication takes place with the spoken word in face-to-face situations (which may be construed to include the telephone). This is also evident in studies and authoritative observations made in other fields of endeavor where a technical, well-established means of group communication has a corollary system of informal face-to-face oral communication. For example, in science the extensive system of printed publication is paralleled by an informal system using the spoken word which, because of its speed, often carries advanced information long before it gets into print.

For many years the underlying oral circuits of communication have been the subject of considerable concern in industrial communication and many people in management have learned that communication is an extremely complex commodity. Executives at the top of a company have many ways to address those who work below—by plant-wide public-address systems, bulletin boards, pamphlets, messages with paychecks, speeches before employee meetings and by many other devices, such as making "the word for the day" available to anyone who wishes to pick up a company telephone and dial a certain number. In other words, there are countless ways for management's messages to go out, but what happens to them on the receiving end and how the reactions come back up through the ranks are matters not so easily controlled regardless of how much money is spent on company communication. As the Hawthorne study discovered many years ago, and as others have enlarged upon since, industrial plant society, like that of the world at large, has its group patterns with leaders who affect communication by informal, face-to-face use of the spoken word.

It is now widely recognized in industry that probably the most important internal communication is associated with the first-line supervisors who are in hourly contact with large numbers of employees. The supervisors are, in effect, a point of separation in a two-step system of communication with lines strung from a company's top to bottom and vice versa. The supervisor, who talks both with employees and management levels above, becomes a message modulator for both what comes down from management and for what moves upward from the employees. The supervisor may himself be a group leader of the kind we have been discussing or if not, he certainly is in direct dealings with such leaders.

As a number of surveys have shown, the supervisor in most industries works very much as an oral communicator in his dozens of daily formal and informal contacts with employees and his frequent meetings with management. The supervisor, therefore, serves his employers as sort of a moderator in a very necessary but indirect conversation between management and employees. It is now widely recognized that in his communication role the supervisor should be a skilled user of the spoken word, both as a talker and a listener.

One study completed at the University of California resulted in a list of nine skills that are sorely needed in this key oral communication of industry. They included: conversational ability, listening, knowledge of human relations from a speech standpoint, conference leadership ability, public-speaking ability, conference participation skills, voice and diction, broad vocabulary and knowledge of parliamentary procedure.

NEEDED: MORE CITIZEN MODERATORS

From all that we know of the social functioning of people in groups, whether they meet in industrial plants or as neighbors along a suburban street, it is evident that their formal and informal leaders have an immense bearing on the quality of persuasion and information going to these groups and in some cases, coming from them. When the groups are all added together in society, the kind and quality of public discussion they represent is very much a product of how their leaders function with the spoken word. These leaders in this context are what might be called our "citizen moderators."

How they moderate our all-important public communication is directly related to the health of a democratic society.

In this age of increasingly complex ideas, when most every citizen is on the target of messages shot by the minute in a thousand ways, we more than ever need good citizen moderators who have the public interest at heart. We desperately require more and more "good men" of words who can rise above the human average to explain, interpret and clarify the terribly difficult issues of the twentieth century and then to guide our citizens in discussions aimed at problem-solving. This idea was expressed at a Duke University Commencement by David D. Henry, President of the University of Illinois.

"As the channels of public debate have become more numerous and far-reaching, so have the questions," said Dr. Henry. "All the old subjects of purely local concern are still with us, but now we also have the tremendous questions of survival in a world of international tension. And the topics range beyond those formerly considered the appropriate agenda of public discussion; they now include science, engineering, space technology, education, economics, intercontinental missiles, the weapons of national defense, international diplomacy.

"With the increased complexity of the issues to be debated by the American people, and with involvement of mass communication, recognized procedures and standards of discussion which emphasize the public interest are more greatly needed than ever before.

"We need voluntary moderators for the public debate of our times, and we should insist that education contribute to their number, their training, and their interest in establishing a [high] standard of public discussion. . . ."

Dr. Henry listed 10 "boundaries" of public discussion that the "voluntary moderator" should promote:

1. The idea at issue should be criticized, not its owner.
2. Each person in a discussion may have purposes as worthy as those of any other.
3. Arrogance of opinion is more to be deplored than arrogant behavior.
4. Rationalization is not logic.
5. Argument from partial or selected facts, without acknowledging the limitation, is dishonest.
6. One must beware of believing only what he wants to hear.
7. One should not be bound by the past, but he should respect it.
8. He who challenges authority should be sure of his own authority to do so.
9. Social progress will be advanced more by consensus than conflict. Each person may choose to be either a part of a problem or of its solution.
10. Participants in a public discussion should seek to identify a public purpose and should be motivated by a public philosophy.

And the Illinois University President concluded that "Public service includes more than public officeholding, more than a public commission. It includes the service of those who seek to maintain the integrity of public discussion."

EDUCATION FOR DISCUSSION

While group leaders, in their tremendously active, vital form of discourse, must read for information, the central element of their communication is an ability to engage in and conduct give-and-take discussions held at any moment with one or a dozen people. Where in education are we training citizens to participate effectively in this kind of leadership discourse? Certainly not in classrooms where the greatest numbers of hours are devoted to reading and to teaching *at* students while they hardly have a chance to develop and utter their thoughts in the kind of free and open discussion that we have bragged about ever since the cracker barrel. The "keep-still" discipline of the three Rs does not promote the spoken skills of our much-needed leadership discourse.

What the social scientist has been telling us about the structure and communication of modern society is perhaps our strongest evidence that we need a modern rhetoric drawn on traditional lines. This knowledge from sociology strongly supports an appeal to educators that they carefully assess the balance of what and how they teach in the development of human communication. Certainly the need for good reading and writing is not diminished but it has to be understood that the written word more and more becomes the repository of knowledge, while the spoken word—as we have just seen in this chapter—increasingly becomes the communication of action on the most basic levels of a democratic society. Until a modern rhetoric returns our pedagogy to a more balanced position between the written and spoken word, the communication of action will continue to suffer, and very much to the danger of our democracy.

XII

The Making
of Participators

IN HIS BOOK *Democracy and Education,* the famous American philosopher and educator, John Dewey, wrote:

"Many of the failures of democratic government are due to the fact that adults are unable to share in joint conference and consultations on social questions and issues. They can neither contribute intelligently nor can they follow and judge the contributions of others. The habits set up in their earlier schooling have not fitted them for this enterprise."

This concern, voiced in 1916, has been repeated frequently and is still heard today.

A 1926 survey of 300 towns in thirty-five states by the National Council of Teachers of English investigated the types of language activities required in daily life. The 2,165 responses led the survey's director, John M. Clapp, to write:

"The schools might well devote more attention to a number of the language activities which, according to the returns, are widely used by persons of the many callings and social groups reporting, and which are reported as giving much difficulty. These activities in particular are: Interviews: word-of-mouth inquiries, reports to a superior, instructions for subordinates, conferences. Conversations: with casual acquaintances, at social gatherings, over the telephone. Public speaking: informal discussion, preparing addresses. Writing:

informal notes and memos for one's self; formal notes of in-
vitation, introduction, etc. Reading: legal documents. Listening: to an interview, a conference or a public meeting."

In 1929 attention was drawn to the results of Paul T.
Rankin's survey in Detroit (described in Chapter I) which
indicated that our talking and listening time far exeeds that
of reading and writing.

Four years later a national survey of secondary education
under the U.S. Office of Education noted a marked difference
between education for written and spoken language. Reporting on this survey, Dora V. Smith pointed out "that the emphasis on written activities in junior high school is more than
double oral composition. In senior high school it is more
than three times as great."

A 1935 report by W. Wilbur Hatfield for the National
Council of Teachers of English stated:

"The actual experiences in communication which go into
the curriculum should be representative of the present experiences of most pupils outside the English class—in other
school classes, in clubs, on the playground, at home, at the
store.

"More time should be spent in oral than in written communication."

In the late 1930s Dora V. Smith made a survey for the
New York Regents in which she again noted: "The average
school in New York follows the practice of giving a mastery
of grammar and mechanics first; then if there is any time left,
it is devoted to writing, and after that, to speech." At the
same time she stressed that, "One of the most pressing problems faced by the schools of New York State today is the improvement of speech and oral expression. . . ."

Dr. Smith found that of the state's eleven teacher-training
institutions supplying 65 per cent of New York's teachers,
only two required courses in speech or oral expression for prospective teachers of English. She concluded: "Above all, it is

imperative to save the program in normal everyday oral expression from meaningless artificiality by integrating it closely with the expressional activities not only of English but of every class in the school, and to give children the opportunity for daily expression under expert guidance in the ordinary social situations of life."

STILL UNBALANCED

Continuing studies and criticisms of adult communication requirements to this day have invariably reflected the need to re-think a curriculum that persists in neglecting the spoken side of language. The Speech Association of America in the mid-1960s put it this way:

"... as a rule teachers prepared within college departments of English have received little instruction in speech and language behavior and the arts of public discussion. The result is an anomaly: a school curriculum in the language arts which assumes instruction in speech but which is taught for the most part by teachers with little or no preparation in speech. The situation has serious consequences. Innumerable graduates of the common schools have practically no knowledge of speech behavior and of the arts of communication, only the most superficial acquaintance with any of the 'literature' of public address and discussion, and no experience at all in rhetorical analysis and appraisal. Large numbers of graduates face a variety of situations requiring ready speech with powers far under their abilities. Such an attenuated and unbalanced treatment of the study of language and the development of language skills is a most serious problem in American education. Teachers of speech and English must recognize their related problems in the curriculum in the English language arts and confront them cooperatively."

To balance the spoken and written words in education is,

of course, a formidable task, for the problem is complexly entwined both with the fundamentals of teaching and learning, and with subject matter for education in and for a democracy. The problem is primarily a responsibility of the language-arts teacher, but is not confined to him by any means; it is also the concern of teachers in all subject areas.

"First of all," to borrow the words of James Bryant Conant, "obviously the teacher disseminates information and it goes without saying that this information should be accurate and significant." It should also go without saying that the teacher's personal, daily task of disseminating information is mainly through the spoken word. He talks to his students and is then guided considerably as to their learning by listening to them. Therefore, as a teacher, one should be skilled in speaking and listening, especially as they apply to conducting a classroom. Such oral-aural facility has to be developed by most people, and teachers are no exception. Their speaking and listening skills require attention in teacher-training institutions.

Secondly, a teacher, regardless of subject, may be a major influence in determining his students' speech habits. This role also demands speaking and listening skills of the teacher as well as knowledge of how to teach them.

SPEECH COMPETENCIES FOR TEACHERS

At Columbia Teachers College, Burton H. Byer completed an extensive doctoral dissertation on speech in education in which he listed "seventeen competencies needed by teachers in order to plan and guide the speaking-listening activities of a democratic classroom." The first five are basic skills which would insure that teachers confront their students with good articulation and pronunciation; a pleasing and effective voice; the necessary projection, posture and gesture, and good spoken vocabulary and grammar. Here in brief summary are some of the major competencies that followed Dr. Byer's first five:

The teacher should know about and be adept at the use of spoken language in teaching. He should, for instance, know the principles and limitations of attempting to transfer a thought from his mind to another person's. He should particularly understand how language, spoken or written, is related to the ability to think. He should be able to recognize in his students' oral discourse the difference between rote learning and the oral exercise of thought. The teacher should also be aware of the pitfalls that might come with too much pride in one's own facile use of oral language, that it may result in a teacher-dominated classroom where students have little opportunity for oral participation.

"Genuine teaching," says Dr. Byer, "must get below the surface of language, and yet it must be accomplished through the use of language. This is why an understanding of how speaking-listening activities fit into the teacher-learning process is an understanding which is cultivated by superior teachers throughout their lives, rather than an understanding which the beginning teacher can bring, full-blown, to his first teaching assignment."

A teacher should have enough acquaintance with the speech profession and its literature to know where to turn for help on speech problems of more than ordinary difficulty. He should be able to recognize the symptomatic differences between speech failings that call for either a speech correctionist or speech teacher. This requires a general understanding of whether speech differences result from psychological, sociological or physiological causes. A comprehension of speech differences is also important to the classroom development of an important democratic principle in listening, i.e., what a person says should come before how he says it.

A teacher, regardless of subject, should know the relationships between good speech and freedom of speech. This knowledge, of course, is essential to classroom conduct based on democratic principles, which in turn reflect upon the democratic values acquired by students. And, needless to say, such understanding is necessary to teach the ways in which speaking-listening activities are the lifeblood of the democratic process.

To foster the much-desired and productive student participation in classroom activities requires a teacher who comprehends and effectively employs a number of important speaking-listening skills. The teacher continually acts as a discussion leader and his oral conduct in this role has considerable influence on whether or not his students will participate well in classroom thought and discourse. Moreover, it has a decided effect on the kind of citizens that the teacher helps develop by general education.

A teacher should come to the classroom with attitudes and appreciations that support the use of good speech in a democracy. These qualities are needed, of course, if he is to lead students to speech improvement and in behalf of its proper and effective use in the democratic process. If the teacher's attitude reveals that he doesn't care about good speech, or if he does not appreciate it when he hears it, his students cannot be expected to respect and cultivate good oral habits.

SPEECH AIMS IN GENERAL

If these and other speech competencies were acquired by all primary and secondary teachers, and especially by those dealing in the language arts, education in general would undoubtedly move in the direction of balancing language skills. Also, the nation's schools would start playing their proper role in building a rhetoric ethically committed to matters of importance rather than a frivolous rhetoric whose chief aim is better sales techniques. When schools make such a basically important contribution to our mother tongue they will have restored the spoken word to its rightful place in human communication, and, in the process, will more fully meet their responsibilities to education for a democracy.

This fulfillment through attention to the spoken word has the potential for at least five major benefits for the general improvement of our language and for a better democratic education. The benefits are largely missing in today's schooling dominated by the written word.

1. APPRECIATION OF FINE SPEECH

The quality of our English language is unlikely to prosper if people do not care about the quality of the spoken word in daily speech.

As toddlers we learn our language aurally, but this teaching process never ends. We are all, to some degree, mimics, we are all somewhat sheeplike. Therefore, it is our inclination to mimic the kind of language most prevalent to our environment. These influences, for most people, are exerted by the spoken word.

Here we have the potential for a vast quality-control system over our mother tongue, but the system, to be set in motion, has to be primed in the nation's schools. With every year of education, kindergarten through twelfth grade and up, we have the opportunity to develop student appreciation for fine speech with lasting effects into adulthood. Not only would our mother tongue be better spoken and written, but those of us who spend so many waking hours listening to radio, television, civic-club speeches, political pleas and conference discussions might exercise our tastes for better speech by exerting pressure for a general upgrading of what we hear.

Today there is little such quality control at work in

America. "To a large extent," says Dominick A. Barbara, psychoanalyst and speech consultant with the American Institute for Psychoanalysis, "we live in an age of conformity. From early childhood we are trained to sit back passively and allow facts from the outside world to pour into our ears with little effort or involvement on our part. We are content mostly to be habitual listeners and permit ourselves to be influenced by some of the great inventions of our time—radio, movies, television.

". . . how often do we ask ourselves what is actually being said and if it has any real meaning to us? How often do we stop to consider how we actually feel about what we have just heard? We prefer to be habitual listeners who listen automatically to sounds and noises with which we have little active self-involvement or real perception."

For years we have heard similar indictments. The low level of radio and television is criticized and those responsible for the electronic "wastelands" point to the mass audience and its low tastes. Political speakers are denounced for their retarded rhetoric and they blame the listener, with reason, for when one tries to uplift such discourse he risks denunciation as an egghead and fuzzy thinker. Advertisers continually aim their spoken words at the lowest common denominator, the mass audience, and rhetorical quality rides the bottom road.

But attacking the problem with pleas and admonishments to those who lower the level of our rhetoric obviously fails. Another approach, a longer but more telling one, is obviously to attack the problem from the audience standpoint.

Little will occur to raise the sights of America's mass audience until something is done to develop its appreciation for good speech. This is not simply a matter of developing taste for fancy, buttered words regardless of meaning. It is that of building appreciation for speech that deals well with ideas of substance.

The nation's teachers have the basic responsibility. The opportunity to work at speech appreciation is present during a great majority of classroom hours. It is possible if teachers insist on speech of quality from students and demonstrate it through speech activities, and, most important of all, through the teachers' own speech.

The foundations for this task need to be laid in our teacher-training institutions. By acquainting future teachers with the opportunities—in daily classroom speech, theatrical activities, movies, radio and television, spoken-word recordings and, especially, the oral interpretation of good literature —schools might be staffed more and more with people prepared to develop the taste for fine speech that can serve, in the long run, as a quality control to the mother tongue.

2. Comfort With Democratic Discourse

If citizens are well prepared to meet their democratic responsibilities, their schooling must acquaint them with, and thereby make them comfortable with, the differences of the spoken word from the written word.

Today many people live in ignorance of what the spoken word can and cannot do. From the ignorance comes a fear of oral language which is much less obvious with the more trusted written word. The phobia ranges from a mild but prevalent distrust of oral discourse (revealed in the apologetic, "Oh, he just says that.") to an unreasonable fear of what many sense as magical properties with which a good speaker can cast a spell to snare the listeners' thinking in favor of his viewpoint. This attitude, of course, is catalyzed in particular by public address.

Alan Reitman, Associate Director of the American Civil Liberties Union, considers that a leading reason for this fear is that public speech is a more open and active form of communication, and therefore more threatening. Public speech, he explains, is used in open assemblies which involve numbers of people rather than the one-to-one relationship of the written word. "In short," adds Reitman, "the reading of a pamphlet is a less active kind of communication—it is something between the author and the individual reader. But public speech, especially controversial speech which antagonizes the community, carries with it the idea of influencing groups of people and thus arouses opposition."

EXPENSIVE DRAWBACKS. This general uneasiness over the spoken word has a number of expensive drawbacks in terms of time, money and, most serious of all, misuse of the public discourse so essential to a democracy.

In our conduct of daily affairs, especially in business, many people live by the motto: "DON'T SAY IT! WRITE IT!" Today's men of affairs, with telephones and endless meetings, are forever talking with one another, but much of the endless stream of spoken words has to be "covered" in writing. Thus America's offices are reservoirs of paperwork that in many instances reflect our distrust for oral communication.

If our speaking and listening habits could be better established through education, and thus used more without fear, the possibilities are considerable for faster, more economical, efficient communication. This is the day when a three-minute, two-way oral communication coast-to-coast by telephone may cost less than the typical piece of business correspondence carrying a one-way message that at best may take twenty-four hours to reach the recipient.

Indeed our uneasiness with the spoken word drives us to embrace the written word which, though we are taught to trust it, is also in shambles. An American Management Association survey found the typical executive spending five hours a day deciphering written reports, correspondence and publications. Four-fifths of the survey's respondents agreed

that much of their effort is wasted, for the material they are
forced to navigate is repetitious, unclear, poorly organized,
late or irrelevant.

DISTRUST OF DEMOCRATIC DISCOURSE. On
a far more serious note, consider how the general distrust of
speech has a detrimental effect on a democratic society where
so much depends on oral language. Think, for instance, of
what it means to political rhetoric, which, like it or not, is a
leading factor in our nation's destiny.

In the minds of millions, the spoken words of all politicians are lies before they are uttered. The more orally facile
political speaker—dealing in truths or falsehoods—is automatically suspect of using magic to snatch a vote. Certainly some
politicians give ample reason for such fear, but to distrust the
rhetoric of all politicians becomes a serious weakness in a
democracy because fear of this kind ends or badly disrupts listening on an intellectual level, which in turn, cuts off the
very considerations that political discourse is supposed to
prompt.

Perhaps the best example in recent history is the political
rhetoric of the late Adlai Stevenson which was widely suspect
by millions of voters though many speech professionals considered it beautiful delivery complementing exemplary oral
content. Great segments of the public analyzed this now-
famous rhetoric as a dangerous quality in the candidate.
They feared it harbored political trickery and were prompted
to shut him off aurally for fear that his "smooth talk" was a
sly coverup for "fuzzy thinking."

This distrust of speech, of course, could not keep Stevenson the candidate from freely speaking his mind, but with
lesser men in our time, the fear has led to the unreasoned
curbing of that cornerstone of democracy, freedom of speech.

For two decades America has provided numerous examples in our attitude toward the Communist speaker or anyone even slightly suspect of being inclined toward the Com-

munist movement. From what has happened one might easily conclude—if he didn't know better—that a Communist has unmatched forensic powers. Five minutes on a soap box—so this peculiar notion goes—and a Communist speaker's persuasive rhetoric can turn an audience against political ideas that have proven themselves superior since the founding of the Republic. Granted that those concerned about Communist persuasion have come close to book burning and have forced the censor's knife upon written material, but nothing in writing seems able to stir up a storm like a controversial speaker.

When such a fear is magnified by the vast power of nationwide television the results can be monstrous and men in the public eye often experience the results. In his book, *Profiles in Courage,* the late President John F. Kennedy said: "Today the challenge of political courage looms larger than ever before. For our everyday life is becoming so saturated with the tremendous power of mass communication that any unpopular or unorthodox course arouses a storm of protest."

FEAR FOR THE YOUNG MIND. Some pregnant examples of the undue fear of spoken word are found, of all places, on many college campuses. While today's college library can be filled with books and magazines carrying controversial ideas, the same thoughts in spoken form can cause a furor.

A University of Minnesota study revealed that a majority of academic administrators give lip service to complete freedom of speech on their campuses, but don't practice it. Three of every four presidents of more than 800 colleges and universities said, "without reservations," that an essential part of academic life is for students to "hear, critically examine and express viewpoints on issues that divide our society."

In practice, however, only one of every four presidents would accept the American Nazi leader, George Lincoln Rockwell as an on-campus speaker. The late Malcolm X would have been rebuffed by nearly the same proportion.

This would also have been true for a speaker representing the Communist Party, like Daniel Rubin. Catholic university presidents were the most restrictive about controversial speakers. Malcolm X could speak on only seven per cent of their campuses, and the Communist Daniel Rubin would have found himself welcomed at only three per cent of the Catholic institutions.

But one doesn't have to visit these college campuses to witness the fear of spoken discourse. It obviously contributes to the general decline of discussion and debate in all walks of American life.

On the one hand individuals dare not enter public discussion for fear that a rebuttal may be personally devastating. On the other hand a prevalent feeling (or possibly it's a rationalization for not getting involved) says that discussions are only "a lot of talk" that never gets anywhere, except to turn into heated arguments tantamount to a fight. In short, there is a general notion that public discussions—while sometimes fun to hear if there's sharp conflict—are affairs to avoid personally.

This odd form of squelch must contribute to the general erosion of the discussion so essential to the foundation of a democratic society. It is not likely to be reversed when a large percentage of citizens are uncomfortable with the spoken word, either as listeners or talkers. Meanwhile, speech that is feared is not free.

The problem behoves America's teachers to provide students with many opportunities to learn about and deal in oral language, especially oral persuasion. The knowledge and experience would certainly lead in the direction of an attitude more trusting and less fearful of oral language. The effort would strike at some of the fears that work against the free and thorough examination of ideas.

While the problem's solutions should largely fall to the language-arts teacher, considerable responsibility still must be taken by all teachers in all subjects. It is during the day-by-day attention to, development of and insistence upon good oral language that teachers can develop good oral skills, thereby reducing the fear now causing difficulties with the most important form of human communication.

3. DEMOCRATIC UNDERSTANDING FROM OUR SPOKEN HERITAGE

While literature courses may well cover our heritage in the written word, a comparable effort with spoken language hardly exists. Yet the spoken heritage of our civilization is equally significant. For instance, the freedom of press that has strengthened America was defined and crystallized by a famous speech in a New York courtroom. The acceptance of the U.S. Constitution in its durable form was most dependent on great speeches made throughout the American colonies by our forefathers. Indeed the turning points of history are often marked by men of the spoken word clearly expressing their ideas at crucial moments.

Also, the machinery of democratic government was forged with the understanding that citizens would be able to contribute to it orally. The revered New England town meeting is a primary example of rule by the people through a spoken forum. Even the allied institution of selectmen to administer town affairs between town meetings depends directly upon oral deliberation as opposed to one-man direction.

Little attention is paid to this oral side of language in most of our schools. Yet in our spoken heritage one finds the most solid elements of the democratic process.

The relationship between leader and followers in a democracy is one of these elements. So many people in today's society see this relationship as that of salesman to customers, i.e., the leader thinks up the ideas and sells them to followers. To the contrary, the true democratic leader is a cultivator of ideas through active oral participation with his followers. In the purest sense of democracy he is a leader of discussion in which he participates with his followers. In this role he must be an able spokesman, but equally important, he must be a good listener who is especially adept at exercising immediate judgment during the give and take of oral discourse.

The follower in the democratic concept also has a large responsibility. Mainly, he must be a fair, but critical listener. He also must be an oral contributor able to express his own ideas and fairly assess those of his colleagues in open discussion.

The speaking-listening concepts of leaders and followers need continual stress and practice in school. Plenty of examples for teaching purposes are found in our speech heritage. Then practice is always possible in the everyday conduct of the classroom—providing teachers are prepared to recognize and take the opportunities they have through daily speech.

Freedom of speech, what it is really about and why it is a stable part of democracy, is of course very much evident in America's spoken heritage. Here also are the examples so necessary for teaching a concept as abstract as speech freedom. While it is being taught, the spoken word, well used in the classrooom, can offer a living demonstration of why freedom of speech is important. Such activity can clearly impress students with the fact that this freedom is not maintained simply that anyone can say anything, but it is preserved because the examination of ideas and opinions is a necessity to human freedom.

DECENTLY AND IN ORDER. For the orderly exercise of speech freedom, our schools have an important responsibility to teach the rules of parliamentary procedure and to give students experience with them. For a democracy such rules are more necessary than many others dwelled upon in the nation's classrooms. They can be far more important to human well-being than the rules of drafting letters, or the rules of grammar as taught through so many school hours.

Here, too, America has an interesting heritage to provide the examples for making this teaching task come alive. The parliamentary rule to "Reconsider," for example, is of American origin. Its disregard in the United States Senate determined that the nation's capital city, Washington, D.C., would be built on the Potomac and not the Susquehanna. In another instance, the "Previous Question" was dramatically moved in the House of Representatives in February 1812 to open the way for an immediate declaration of war against England.

With concern for parliamentary procedure in America, James Madison wrote to Thomas Jefferson in 1787: "In framing a government which is to be administered by men over men, the great difficulty lies in this: you must first enable the government to control the governed; and in the next place oblige it to control itself."

Long before Madison, St. Paul speaking to the Corinthians put the problem most succinctly: "Let all things be done decently and in order."

To have parliamentary order at all levels of a democracy is the responsibility of educators, but one only has to attend a few of the nation's daily meetings to recognize that the responsibility is not met. Meanwhile, daily classroom conduct offers ample opportunity to teach the necessary rudiments of using the spoken word "decently and in order."

THE SPOKEN STRUCTURE OF GOVERNMENT. As students learn the basic elements of the spoken word in a democracy, they should also be informed of how they apply in the conduct of government from the local to national level. They should learn of their speaking-listening responsibilities in future voting decisions. And they should comprehend the role that discussion and debate should play in legislative efforts from the town meeting to the halls of the U.S. Congress.

Most important of the citizen's direct responsibilities with the spoken word is that of serving on a jury. It should be the most zealously held right of citizens in a democracy, but how many people are truly prepared for such duty? It chiefly requires the critical skills of listening which are almost completely ignored in American education, though we definitely know they are subject to development and improvement.

In addition to the listening skill, the juror should know how the principles of debate are put to work by courtroom attorneys. Furthermore, the American juryman should come from his general education with some ideas of the rules of speech in a courtroom. And central to his knowledge of the jury and justice should be basic concepts of how speaking and listening need to be carefully applied in order to arrive at the truth, as opposed to one side winning right or wrong.

The making of future jurors certainly is the concern of our teachers. Again, in their classrooms, are found daily opportunities to build the skills and knowledge that our courts need in citizens who deal in justice.

HEURISTIC VS. ERISTIC. By proper attention to our spoken heritage, educators have a chance to make a tremendous contribution to society if only they impart one notion to the future citizen: Democracy has functioned best when heuristic argument is the prevalent form of discourse. Today, eristic argument is in the lead.

4. Orally Committed People

If schools are to produce citizens who can add favorably to democratic society, students, even from the earliest grades, must trade in ideas of substance. Such trade is not likely to amount to much if the most used medium of communication, the spoken word, is not skillfully fostered by teachers. If education is to be more than the propagandization of pupils, classrooms, now widely marked by the massive silence of student uninvolvement, must become the scene of young people talking, not only to teachers, but mainly to each other, about things that matter. Education would then benefit from the rhetorical practice of the "dialogue" which has played a crucial role developing the men of ideas who have given structural substance to Western civilization.

COMMITTED AND ARTICULATE. Two teacher qualities seem necessary to the classroom discussion of ideas of substance:

First, we need teachers committed to important ideas. As pointed out by Michael P. Walsh, S.J., President of Boston College, teachers for a half century "have been priding themselves in their ability to employ a rhetoric of noncommitment," while also taking pride in a "reputation of objectivity."

"Yet," asks Father Walsh, "isn't there something fundamentally more honest in proclaiming 'These are my beliefs; these are what I teach,' than in pretending to teach no values, which is really a way of denying all values?"

This concern was also voiced by the president of another Catholic institution, Sister Margaret of Trinity College, speaking before the National Catholic Educational Association. She urged that students be educated for militancy and controversy rather than submission and conformity. She asked: "Should we not in our education be developing people with the courage of commitment to dissent and involvement?

"Too often today people in our schools [teachers] are more propagandists than educators and so our students never do develop to the point where they make a difference."

Second, we need teachers equipped to encourage and cultivate the pupil dialogue so important to educating citizens ethically committed to the important issues of our times. Today's pedagogy is not noted for people with training and experience for handling the spoken interplay of important ideas, which, in turn, means they are unable to nurture discussion of the same among their youngsters.

Until our teacher-training institutions develop a dialogue of ideas that matter, as well as the spoken skills for effectively handling such discourse, we are unlikely to see many true educators as opposed to the pedagogical propagandists recognized by Sister Margaret.

WHAT DO THEY SAY? If we had teachers to foster a continuing educational dialogue among students what would they talk about? Actually, subjects are found at the tips of youngsters' tongues from kindergarten up—though the higher a pupil goes through the grades the more discouraged he may become about the chances of airing these topics. In the earliest grades, for example, the question of "What is fair?" is forever on the minds of youngsters. Consider all the possibilities of that question. What is fair for me on the playground? And what is fair for the other kids? What is fair about the line at the cafeteria? Why is fairness involved with cheating and stealing? Is it fair to put people in jail? Is it fair to talk behind people's back? Is it fair to make everyone go to school?

"The question of what is fair is forever on the minds of young people," says Alice Rothschild who, for many years, taught second-graders in New York's Dalton School and is now a children's-book author. "Permitting, encouraging and helping children talk about what bothers them is extremely important to their development of ideas. The subject of fairness is forever bothering them."

As children advance through the grades, the educational dialogue of course should grow broader and deeper. Virgil L. Baker and Ralph T. Eubanks of the University of Arkansas feel that teachers must lead their students in the discussion of topics and issues that involve them in questions of values in art, literature, political science, ethics, religion, history and contemporary public affairs. This approach, say the two teachers, puts rhetorical education "into the business of helping students make wise choices in the realm of human values with the ultimate goal that of creating human excellence, both public and private . . ."

Through it all, say Drs. Baker and Eubanks, a teacher should be a fair but stern critic of student discussions and statements of ideas and values, at the same time abandoning the "nerveless contention" that the valid use of such criticism is being a propagandizer. Teachers should also insist that their student dialogues be based on research of quality, and in so doing they will discover "the best antidote to the ill-devised proposal, the surest means of infusing soberness into . . . students' counsels on public questions." And through it all teachers must make it clear that a rhetorical education is more than a gimmick for advancing a career, but instead that "it helps to make of him [the student] a fully civilized human being."

NOTHING UNDISCUSSED. When our educationists apply themselves to the development of teachers who themselves can foster and play a part in a continuing dialogue of important values, with and among their students, we may be headed on a truer course toward the kind of a society which can be more rightfully described as "democratic."

"The goal toward which Western society moves," says Robert Maynard Hutchins, former president of the University of Chicago, "is the Civilization of the Dialogue. The spirit of Western civilization is the spirit of inquiry. Its dominant element is the *Logos*. Nothing is to remain undiscussed. No proposition is to be left unexamined. The exchange of ideas is held to be the path to the realization of the potentialities of the race."

5. DEFENSE AGAINST A DEMAGOGUE

In a nation of free speech where the great inventions of our time shower us all with endless storms of spoken persuasion, it would seem that a required course somewhere in school should treat with "How to Recognize a Demagogue." Such a course would essentially cover the skills of critical listening. In a society where free speech, if it is to remain free, must run the risk of a demagogue, the main defense is found in the listener.

The former Nazi youth leader, now a California teacher of speech, Fred L. Casmir, says: "In the long run the only way in which the rise of demagogues, the persuaders of the masses, can be prevented, is the development of our own stringent rules for listening and observing, and by demanding correct information from the mass-information media at all times. The responsibility of the listener, therefore, must be stressed."

If we now look to see if our teachers are laying such stress, we find the defenses against a demagogue are down. Many of us can't imagine that listening, like reading, is a skill that educators can develop as part of a student's intellectual equipment. Formal attention to listening has, until recent years, been entirely foreign to American schools. While listening is now a much discussed topic in American education, not too much is done about it in primary or secondary education.

CRITICAL LISTENING TESTED. Some interesting investigations with college students have shown that (1) they have been ill prepared in previous schooling for critical listening, and (2) courses and experience in speech and listening can develop the discipline.

At the University of Iowa, Lawrence W. Brewster tested 323 students on their critical ability in listening to speeches on controversial subjects deliberately composed with arguments weak in supporting evidence. Analysis of the students' written results revealed that most of the students, when asked to write "commentaries" on what they heard, wrote only summaries. The few who did write what could rightfully be called commentaries were "able to make more correct judgments as to whether certain statements were actually made or implied in a speech and whether those statements, if made, were supported by evidence."

In research conducted by Ellwood R. Tame at the University of Denver, 400 contest debaters and discussants from forty-four colleges and universities were tested for three factors: (1) logical reasoning, (2) recognition of presumption and burden of proof in problems, and (3) reflective thinking. The results were compared with the students' records in discussions and debates. Those who excelled in the speech contests demonstrated the greatest ability in critical thinking. Those with the least debating experience indicated the least ability in critical thinking.

An earlier study by Winston L. Brembeck at the University of Wisconsin found that a semester course in argumentation improves critical thinking ability, and that a college student's scores on a critical thinking test were favorably influenced by past debating experience.

Our best teachers of speech have a good explanation for such results. For instance: "Original speechmaking and discussion," says Elbert Harrington, Dean of the College of Liberal Arts and Sciences at the University of North Dakota, "call for the evaluation of data, the establishment of relationships among ideas and a recognition of the strength and weakness of assumptions which underlie ideas or whole systems of thought. The interpretation of a play or selection of literature rests on a thorough understanding of meaning. Good speech is fundamentally a thinking process."

THE GREAT RHETORICAL PROOFS. In building defenses against demagoguery, knowledge of speech structure is a valuable ingredient for critical listening. For this reason, it should be made certain that our students somewhere in their education learn of the rhetorical proofs listed by Aristotle. With such understanding, they are more likely to use them with integrity in speech, and recognize their abuse by others.

If only one of these proofs could be chosen for today's curriculum it undoubtedly should be *ethical* proof. Its understanding is especially important today if we are to remain secure against a demagogue.

Ethical proof is what a speaker presents his audience, not through words, but through the external effects that he offers with those words. An individual, for instance, is introduced with the ethical proof that he is the leading authority on such and such a subject, thereby the listener who accepts that proof may feel free to accept the speaker's words. Of course, a listener has the responsibility of assessing such proof, but few Americans have ever heard of ethical proof, which may explain why it is one of the most abused elements of today's public speech.

It is the success of a movie actor throwing his popular weight behind a Presidential candidate. It is the millionaire's money offered as proof that he is an authority on all matters political and otherwise. Most serious, ethical proof is the popular notion that if a person's voice is broadcast on radio or television, he has to be speaking the truth.

"The reason *ethical* proof is a troublesome question for rhetoricians," says Professor Harrington at North Dakota, "is that it can be so easily abused. Modern means of communication and methods of advertising can create and magnify ethical qualities to the point where a mediocre man becomes the leader, or the demagogue becomes the hero. The audience is usually denied the opportunity to meet the speaker face to face, a situation which, when it existed, was healthy. Television has helped some, but it has its limitations in permitting the audience to estimate the true ethical qualities of a speaker."

OPPORTUNITY FOR BETTER LISTENING. But no audience is likely to handle such problems well until our schools make substantial efforts toward listening improvement. For some time we have known that listening as a skill can be taught. A study completed in 1948 at the University of Iowa by Ralph G. Nichols—still considered one of the most thorough analyses of the listening process—revealed a number of factors pointing toward the possibilities for teaching listening. The most fascinating was the idea that we can, in terms of words per minute, think much faster than even the fastest talker can speak. In this differential Dr. Nichols saw the opportunity to develop intellectual skills that could help a listener better comprehend and assess what he hears. In this process he also saw the opportunity for the kind of critical listening so essential to the recognition of a demagogue.

Dr. Nichols, now at the University of Minnesota, has said that if only we could educate in behalf of more critical listening, two great benefits would be ours:

"Life will be easier for the man who talks to persuade us to take action for our own good and for that of our fellow men.

"The man who uses oral persuasion for less honorable reasons will find his task becoming increasingly difficult."

The benefits of a citizenry better educated in the spoken word are unlikely to be realized unless we can have a major, concerted effort among educators to balance the spoken-written ingredients of teaching our own language. Experience clearly shows us that this cannot be accomplished with one educational interest group. It must be motivated on high by educators of many callings, as well as people from government, business and science, who see the need in a democracy for cultivating quality and integrity in the medium of human communication that is the most used, most important part of our language.

XIII

Can Communication
Teachers Communicate?

SINCE WORLD WAR II—with a powerful assist from the first
Russian Sputnik—American educators have been making curriculum changes that, in some subject areas and in some
schools, supposedly bring education closer to modern requirements. The effort, noted for its advances in mathematics
and science, has been slow to move into the humanities, but
is now doing so. This move, plus the fact that large amounts
of public and private funds have become available for education, provide an opportunity to take an objective, critical
look at the training we offer toward the improvement of
human communication. Such a look in today's world would
demand serious consideration of the imbalance between the
spoken and written forms of communication. To bring the
two into their proper perspective in relation to our needs in a
modern democracy is likely to be one factor important to its
very survival.

Education, as now organized, makes the problem of a
comprehensive approach to the teaching of human communication extremely complex because the learning of our
mother tongue—formally and informally—is a badly com-
partmentalized affair. The communication authorities who
occupy these compartments are good at inward communication (understanding themselves) but they apparently suffer a

block to outward communication (understanding others).

For many years, it seems obvious, the teachers of English, clinging to troubled educational programs tied to the written word, have barred the door to those who might have shown the way to teaching language as an integrated whole. Otherwise, the methods always favoring reading and writing might have been more effectively questioned.

On the other hand one cannot long consider the teachers of speech without thinking that they too have failed at the communicative art at which they should be masters. To most people, and this includes a great many teachers, the word "speech" used in reference to an academic subject, conveys about as much meaning as would the term stated in Chinese. If the phrase "public speaking" is substituted one can find some understanding, though it is only a part of what the teachers of speech consider the best course for a modern rhetoric. This bleak public understanding is more likely to have come from independent sources of adult instruction where techniques of voice and gesture are offered to the neglect of oral content. In other words, the most powerful promotion of oral improvement in America is often the product of people whose true effectiveness (and even integrity) is questioned most severely by leaders in the academic field of speech.

In the communication vineyard we also find linguists, semanticists, group dynamicists, information theorists, human relationists and others who in different ways have ideas for improving our ability to transfer thoughts between human minds. They too have important contributions to make toward the effective teaching of our own language. But while many of their ideas are worthwhile, seldom are they used effectively in schools because they have not been fitted into the curriculums in a meaningful, practical fashion.

And through it all, our students encounter many other language teachers who are not labeled as such, nor intended to be, but who are powerful molders of the mother tongue.

They include all teachers, from science and mathematics to art and driver education. Also included are parents, relatives, friends and the ubiquitous voices of radio and television. Like it or not, they are all language teachers and in many cases are far more potent than those who put the top claims on the job.

ALL TEACHERS, NO DIRECTION

In sum total, a great many people with different ideas, motives and abilities are playing a role in teaching English, directly or indirectly, for good or bad, without any one individual knowing the total effect on the language-learning picture.

For a simple example, a teacher of English, heavily committed to the written word, may work three hours a day at what he considers English-language improvement for his students, only to have his wards return to their homes where parents, along with radio and television, butcher what happened in school. The teacher, as admirable as his efforts may be, is working with a medium that is undoubtedly far less potent as a language-learning tool than the oral medium promoting poor habits at home.

We know that the educational results with our own language are less than admirable, but this is likely to continue until our one language-teaching hand knows what the other is doing and how together they may become effective toward the common goal of improving the learning and use of the mother tongue. For such understanding, which might lead to effective action, a comprehensive look at our own language-learning problem is past due. It is not a look that can be accomplished objectively and well by any one of the disciplines now engaged in teaching what amounts to communication skills. The mainstays in the field, the teachers of English, for instance, see the learning of English through eyes conditioned from years of struggle with the first two Rs and though they are now trying through what started out as Project English, it may be expecting too much that they should be able, with complete objectivity, to find the best avenues for learning our own language. Also, when one discipline has the sole responsibility, there is more chance of the results being subjectively influenced to their detriment by vested interests which range from expensive investments in language-arts textbooks to pet projects of individual teachers.

A CONFERENCE ON THE MOTHER TONGUE

Long past due is a highly placed, concerted effort in the order of a "White House Conference" to consider the health of the mother tongue. If not of White House origin, such a conference might be at the instigation of the Secretary of Health, Education and Welfare. As such conferences have proven in other fields, many people with a variety of thoughts and possible contributions can be drawn together to focus upon a continuing and concerted consideration of an important common problem. And what could be more important than the health of our mother tongue, which, as this book has tried to reveal, suffers serious disabilities that are reflected in the conduct of our most important affairs, in government, science, education, business, religion, the family and all the daily human contacts that form the fibers of a whole society.

First, in the overall sense, a conference on the mother tongue might lead to the elemental definition of our language-learning problem—not as now seen by the English teacher, the speech teacher, the semanticist, the linguist or any other specialist, but the composite problem of how to teach effective, responsible communication with our language for our time. It is doubtful that this problem has been truly defined. Obviously many people feel it is strictly a matter of reading improvement, or some say that good thinking is the main ingredient, or others that it is only a matter of improving human relations. But the true problem's definition undoubtedly needs the cooperative thought of many people from different areas of concern for communication.

Second, a conference of enough magnitude might have the force to draw together for the common purpose all existing knowledge of human communication. It is safe to say that most teachers of our own language lack even the most important pieces of knowledge which could make their work more effective. A major conference might start the cross-fertilization of ideas which could bring untold benefits to our learning the mother tongue. Neurologists, for example, may very well have some unused keys to the teaching of reading and listening. Business-training executives may have important ideas on the communication needs of a large percentage of today's college graduates. Child-development authorities may have vital thoughts on how the earliest beginnings of language-learning in the home may be improved to the benefit of that in school and eventually in adult communication. Such cross-fertilization of ideas might reduce wasted time and effort in language-learning which must result from today's fractured approach that fails to assemble everything we know and put it to work in a practical way.

Third, a conference with enough scope might point to multidisciplined research and study leading toward the improvement of the mother tongue. In the effort to develop our language abilities as a whole, rather than as separate, loosely related skills, research drawing upon many and all areas of pertinent knowledge would undoubtedly produce results to benefit all human communication. For example, research conducted by a neurologist, psychologist and a speech specialist might further define the speech and listening process, how they relate to other communication skills and how they can be better put to work in the whole language-learning process.

More than anything else, a major conference on the mother tongue might lead to a better-balanced consideration of the spoken and written mediums to produce the broader language-oriented thinking which can apply all that we know to train people to use English—whether in reading, speaking, listening, or writing—as effective communication to the best advantage of everyone in a democratic society.

SOME POSSIBILITIES

A major conference on the mother tongue would deal with many problems. A number of them have been discussed in earlier chapters. Here in summary, and at random, is a selection of these problems. Each is followed by a rhetorical question that a major conference might consider in relation to the spoken word.

• The moment-by-moment use of oral language while "thinking on one's feet" is a common ingredient of teaching in any subject. Is it excusable that a large percentage of our teachers and prospective teachers have proceeded through their entire education with hardly an hour of formal oral improvement?

• Every student in every class, through both his listening and speaking, is an ever-present prospect for language improvement. Would it not be wise to consider every teacher in our schools a language teacher by oral methods and give him training to improve upon that task as a natural byproduct of everything else he does?

• The teachers of foreign languages and of English as a second language have found their total efforts, including reading, most effective when groundwork is laid with the spoken word followed by work in the written medium. Why isn't this true in teaching English as a first language? Is it possible that the proper cultivation of oral abilities might build foundations beneficial to both reading and writing?

• Good communication requires that the parties involved be sensitive to how the choice of words and their organization affect other people. It is not hard to understand how this kind of sensitivity is likely to be better nourished and impressed upon students through the living give-and-take of oral activity than by written exercise. Is it possible that such sensitivity developed in oral discussion might transfer itself to the use and to the benefit of written language?

• If clarity of thought and purpose is not present in a sender's message the resulting difficulties are usually evident in the person receiving the communication. This reaction, serving as feedback, can be an impressive tool for developing sensitivity to the use of words with clarity. The spoken word, with its immediate and often powerful feedback from listener to speaker, certainly seems to offer more possibilities for this educational tool than the written word where the receiver's reactions are often remote in time and place. Why can't this difference favoring oral exercise be better capitalized upon in schools in behalf of better composition, both spoken and written?

• Testing has shown that students comprehend poetry better when they hear it read aloud than when they read it silently. In the same vein, it stands to reason that drama, which is written for actors to speak, is likely to be more enjoyed and better understood when heard than when read silently. Surveys of teacher-training institutions indicate that oral interpretation, which is the basis for good oral reading, is not stressed among prospective teachers of English. Should not all teachers receive such training inasmuch as their work continually calls for reading aloud?

• Teachers quite naturally think of themselves as purveyors of information, but seem to have thought very little of themselves as receivers of information from the children they teach. Listening by a teacher may be a tool, especially in the language arts, equally important as many teacher-to-pupil communications. If this is so, should not all teachers and prospective teachers be trained in listening skills for the classroom?

• It is widely acknowledged that the oral discourse between parents and children beginning in infanthood is a determining factor in the youngster's language development. Flora Rheta Schrieber of the New School for Social Research, put it this way: "... the Johnnies in my classroom ... can't read (latest gloomy statistic—35 per cent of our children are seriously retarded in reading), write or spell, and lag in vocabulary ... because their childhoods have too often been barren of words. Johnny's first contact is with language spoken to him. When this first encounter has been abortive, he never learns to love words, never begins his journey of discovery with them. And that's why he is not excited about reading, writing or anything else that has to do with words." Is it possible that, in behalf of upgrading language in general, prospective parents, either as students in school or as adults preparing for parenthood, could be helped more than they are to carry out their inherited duty of orally teaching children their first use of language?

• The dialogue between teacher and student, and between student and student is a concept gaining attention in education. It obviously has many possibilities for helping students to think and act together. To take educational advantage of the dialogue as a modern learning tool, should not teachers and teacher training institutions explore and consider some historically successful oral methods used by teachers who date back a couple of thousand years?

• It is hardly questionable that good thinking cultivates good language, but a more exciting hypothesis is that the cultivation of good language produces good thinking. In this vein there are indications that environmental factors, of which language is certainly a most important one, have a direct effect on the development of a child's intelligence.

Since spoken language is the medium most used, wouldn't it be wise to explore the possible thought benefits of stressing oral improvement, especially among our youngest children?

• In the general neglect of the spoken word in education it is often forgotten that our civilization has a heritage in oratory as well as in literature. Why wouldn't an understanding of the oral part of our history—which for more recent times can actually be heard from recordings—help students better comprehend the power of speech, the key role it plays in a democratic society and how to use it effectively and responsibly themselves?

• The general lack of participation in our most important affairs is being deplored by educators, the clergy, politicians and many others. But few seem to consider that a major deterrent is the lack of oral skill. We already know from today's speech education that this can be remedied. Why is it that schools do not consider it more vigorously?

• There are indications that the open-mindedness so necessary to freedom of speech is promoted by the active give-and-take of oral discussions among students. Can we afford to ignore that students, in addition to what they read about freedom of speech, might learn the most about it in oral confrontation on important, controversial topics?

• Freedom of speech cannot be enjoyed without the risks of demagoguery, which, as history has proven, is most often exercised by the spoken word. This risk can be reduced if future citizens learn the skills of critical listening and the rudiments of responsible persuasion. Isn't this a number-one task of language education in a democracy?

• We are frequently told that by public demand the stage, the movies and radio and television provide us with a vast cultural "wasteland." How can educators develop a general sense of appreciation for better fare in these spoken word media and thereby create a public demand for a more commendable cultural climate?

• In a democracy we stress equality which very much depends upon the judgment of ideas independent of individual differences such as manner of dress, skin color, economic status and speech disabilities. The development of such objective judgment is certainly not promoted by written exercise as readily as by oral methods, especially through small group discussions among students. But observers of today's teachers and their training institutions have been painfully aware of how good discussion is not one of their fortes. What can be done to foster it among practicing teachers and in the training of future teachers?

• In the purest sense, the task of a democratic leader is not to sell his ideas to his followers, but to promote their participation in decisions made for the common good. The sense of this crucial democratic requirement certainly cannot be taught as well in education through written exercise as through the oral discussion of subjects that matter to students. How can this concept be conveyed to future citizens effectively if we continue to slight the spoken word in education?

These problems have been with us for a long time and we are already suffering their disturbing results. Time is not lessening their effects, but instead it brings innovations that make the problems more acute. They warrant attention brought to bear by the nation's leaders.

How we communicate with one another through daily speech is inseparable from what we are, what we do, and what we become.

BIBLIOGRAPHY

Page numbers in brackets indicate where references apply to text.

Chapter I

[*6*]

RANKIN, PAUL T. "Listening Ability," Proceedings of the Ohio State Educational Conference, Ohio State University, Columbus, 1939, pp. 172–183.

[*7*]

Data on telephones and their use obtained from AMERICAN TEL. & TEL. CO., N.Y., 1965.

[*7*]

KAPPEL, FREDERICK R. "Communication Today and Tomorrow," Speech, October 18, 1960. Obtained from AMERICAN TEL. & TEL. CO., N.Y.

[*8*]

GOULD, JACK. "Television: A Wild Time in Store for Prime Time," *The New York Times,* Jan. 11, 1965.

[*8*]

BAXTER, WILLIAM S. "Television Changes Life for the Young," Excerpt from Ph.D. dissertation, University of Iowa, 1960, in *Broadcasting,* Oct. 24, 1961.

[*9*]

HAMMER, ALEXANDER R. "New Hotels Rely on Conventions," *The New York Times,* June 26, 1963.

[*9*]

WHYTE, WILLIAM H., JR., "America's Arch Villain," *Fortune,* April, 1956.

Chapter II

[*12*]

JONES, JAMES L., "Juries, Jargon, and Justice," *Today's Speech,* April, 1964.

[*12*]
"Fighting Prosecutor, Maurice Nadjari," *The New York Times,* Jan. 9, 1965.

[*13*]
"Talks on American Law." Series of Broadcasts to Foreign Audiences by Members of the Harvard Law School Faculty, Ed. Harold J. Berman. New York, 1961. (Paperback)

[*13*]
NIZER, LOUIS, *Thinking on Your Feet.* New York, 1963. (Paperback)

[*14*]
ROVERE, RICHARD, "The Minds of Barry Goldwater," *Harper's* Magazine, Sept., 1964.

[*15*]
OBERDORFER, DON. "Vast Ghostland of Washington," *The New York Times Magazine,* April 26, 1964.

[*15*]
"Senate Approves $1.1 Billion in Aid for Appalachia," *The New York Times,* Feb. 2, 1965.

[*15*]
"House Franck Case Will Receive Hearing Before Supreme Court," *The New York Times,* Jan. 26, 1965.

[*16*]
NORRIS, JOHN G. "House Votes $47 Billion Defense Measure, 410-1." *The Washington Post,* June 27, 1963.

[*16*]
LYONS, LOUIS M. "Wanted: Watchmen for Fourth Estate," *The Nation,* Jan. 18, 1965.

[*17*]
CROSBY, JOHN. "Conformity Rules," New York *Herald Tribune,* May 11, 1962.

[*17*]
HUMPHREY, HUBERT H. "A Nuclear Test Ban and National Security," *Congressional Record,* March 7, 1963.

[*17*]
CROSBY, JOHN, "The Disappearance of Dissent," New York *Herald Tribune,* May 9, 1962.

[*17*]
CLARK, JOSEPH S., U.S. Senator from Pennsylvania. "Congress Fails to Keep Pace With The Times," Statement issued from his office, Washington, D.C., Feb. 20, 1963.

[*19*]
MICCICHE, S. J. "Legislators Admit Image is Poor," The Boston
Globe, Oct. 10, 1963.

[*19*]
"Defending the Constitution," Editorial in *The New York Times,*
May 24, 1963.

[*20*]
BRODER, DAVID S. "Great Speeches Aren't Necessarily Good Politics,"
The New York Times Magazine, March 29, 1964, p. 25.

[*20*]
WHITE, THEODORE. *The Making of A President,* New York, 1961.

[*20*]
The Speeches of John F. Kennedy, Presidential Campaign, 1960,
Government Printing Office, 1961.

[*20*]
*The Speeches of Vice President Richard M. Nixon, Presidential
Campaign, 1960,* Government Printing Office, 1961.

[*20*]
*The Joint Appearances of Senator John F. Kennedy and Vice Presi-
dent Richard M. Nixon, Presidential Campaign, 1960,* Government
Printing Office, 1961.

[*21*]
LAZARASFELD, PAUL; BERELSON, BERNARD and GAUDET, HAZEL, *People's Choice,* Columbia University Press, 1948.

[*22*]
LAZARASFELD, PAUL; BERELSON, BERNARD and McPHEE, WILLIAM.
Voting. The University of Chicago Press, 1954.

[*22*]
"Debates, 1960," *Quarterly Journal of Speech,* April, 1963.

[*22*]
FREELY, AUSTIN. "The Presidential Debates and the Speech Profession." *Quarterly Journal of Speech,* Feb., 1961.

[*22*]
LIPPMANN, WALTER. "His Last Ploy," New York *Herald Tribune,*
Oct. 27, 1964.

[*24*]
RESTON, JAMES. "A Few Sour Reflections on the Campaign," *The
New York Times,* Oct. 30, 1964.

[*24*]
"The Campaign Feeds on Itself," New York *Herald Tribune,*
Oct. 23, 1964.

[24]
LAWRENCE, DAVID L. "The Power of Good Speech," *Today's Speech,* Feb., 1963.

[24]
ZELKO, HAROLD P. and O'BRIEN, HAROLD J. *Management-Employee Communication in Action,* Cleveland, 1957, Preface.

[24]
ZELKO, HAROLD P. "Trends in Oral Communication in Business and Industry," *Journal of Communication,* Vol. 12, 1962.

[25]
HASCH, JACK J. "Your Voice Can Save You Time and Money," *Today's Speech,* Sept., 1962.

[26]
"What Communication Means to Top Management," *Management Review,* May, 1955.

[27]
An Operations Research Study of the Scientific Activity of Chemists, Operations Research Group, Case Institute of Technology, 1958.

[28]
SULLIVAN, WALTER. Article on Science Information, *The New York Times,* Dec. 25, 1961, p. 1.

[29]
Science, Government, and Information. A Report of The President's Science Advisory Committee, The White House, Jan. 10, 1963.

[30]
ABELSON, PHILIP H. "Some Needed Reforms," *Science,* May 10, 1963.

[32]
BYER, BURTON H. "Speech in Teacher Education," unpublished dissertation for Doctor of Ed. Degree, Teachers College, Columbia University, 1957.

[33]
TOLLIVER, CRANNELL. "Speech Training Needs of Public School Teachers," *Speech Monographs,* 1953.

[33]
CAIN, WENDELL. "Speech Proficiency as a Factor in Teacher Certification," *Speech Monographs,* June 1956, p. 151.

[33]
The National Interest and The Teaching of English, The National Council of Teachers of English, 1961.

[33]
ERICKSON, MARCELINE. "Course Preparation in Colleges and Univer-

sities of the Central States for Speech Teachers-To-Be in Secondary
Schools," Unpublished study completed at Mankato (Minn.) State
College, 1962.

[35]

KOERNER, JAMES D. *The Miseducation of American Teachers.* Cambridge, 1963, p. 82.

[36]

"Teachers and Youth Leaders." Report of the Committee appointed
by the President of the Board of Education to Consider the Supply,
Recruitment and Training of Teachers and Youth Leaders, London:
His Majesty's Stationery Office, 1944, p. 66.

Chapter III

[37]

YOUNG, J. Z. *Doubt and Certainty in Science.* The BBC Reith Lectures, 1950, Published, 1951, Republished, New York, 1960. (Paperback)

[38]

LANGER, SUSANNE K. "The Origins of Speech and Its Communicative Function," *Quarterly Journal of Speech,* April, 1960.

[38]

WOOLDRIDGE, DEAN E. *The Machinery of the Brain,* New York, 1963.
(Paperback)

[39]

PENFIELD, WILDER. "The Uncommitted Cortex, The Child's Changing Brain." *Atlantic* Magazine, July, 1964.

[39]

PENFIELD, W. and ROBERTS, L. *Speech and Brain Mechanisms,*
Princeton University Press, 1959.

[45]

DENES, PETER B. and PINSON, ELLIOT N. *The Speech Chain, The
Physics and Biology of Spoken Language,* Bell Telephone Laboratories,
Inc., 1963.

[45]

CHERRY, COLIN. *On Human Communication,* New York, 1961,
(Paperback), p. 69.

Chapter IV

[47]

NICHOLS, RALPH G. "Factors Accounting for Differences in Comprehension of Materials Presented Orally in the Classroom," Unpublished doctor's dissertation, State University of Iowa, 1948.

[47]
NICHOLS, RALPH G., "Factors in Listening Comprehension." *Speech Monographs,* XV, No. 2, 1948.

[48]
FRENCH, NORMAN R., CARTER, CHARLES W., and KOENIG, WALTER, JR. "The Words and Sounds of Telephone Conversations," *Bell System Technical Journal,* April, 1930.

[48]
HOROWITZ, MILTON W. "Writing and Speaking: Two Gateways to the Mind," *Today's Speech,* April, 1964.

[51]
SHAW, HARRY, *Punctuate It Right,* New York, 1963.

[53]
"Psychiatrist Tells How Men Talk Without Words," New York *Herald Tribune,* Aug. 26, 1956.

[53]
HARMS, L. S., "Listener Judgements of Status Cues in Speech." *Quarterly Journal of Speech,* April, 1961.

[53]
LANG, WILLIAM C., "Public Address as a Force in History," *Quarterly Journal of Speech,* Feb. 1951.

[54]
MAZO, EARL, *The Great Debates,* Papers published by the Center for the Study of Democratic Institutions, Santa Barbara, Calif., 1962.

[56]
WIEMAN, HENRY NELSON, "Speech in the Existential Situation," *Quarterly Journal of Speech,* April, 1961.

[58]
SHIRLEY, MARY M., "The First Two Years: A Study of Twenty-five Babies," Vol. II. *Child Monograph Series.* No. 7. Minneapolis: University of Minnesota Press, 1933.

[59]
BURKE, THOMAS, Introduction to *The Ecstasies of Thomas De Quincey.*

[59]
POE, EDGAR ALLAN, "Marginalia."

Chapter V

[62]
"Innovation and Experiment in Education," A Progress Report of

the Panel on Educational Research and Development, Government Printing Office, Washington, D.C., 1964.

[*64*]

GLEASON, H. A., JR., "What Grammar?" *Harvard Educational Review*, Spring, 1964.

[*64*]

ONG, WALTER J., "Grammar Today: Structure in A Vocal World," *Quarterly Journal of Speech*, Dec. 1957.

[*65*]

MAYER, MARTIN, *The Schools*, New York, 1961, p. 198.

[*66*]

BOLINGER, DWIGHT L., "Around the Edge of Language Intonation," *Harvard Educational Review*, Spring, 1964.

[*66*]

POSTAL, PAUL M., "Underlying and Superficial Linguistic Structure," *Harvard Educational Review*, Spring, 1964.

[*67*]

SCHILLER, ANDREW, "The Coming Revolution in Teaching English," *Harper's* Magazine, Oct., 1964.

[*68*]

GOLDEN, RUTH I., "Ways to Improve Oral Communication of Culturally Different Youth," U.S. Office of Education Bulletin, 1964, No. 5, *Improving English Skills of Culturally Different Youth in Large Cities*, p. 100.

[*68*]

BELLOWS, F. L., *The Techniques of Language Teaching*, New York, 1961.

[*68*]

HECHINGER, FRED M., "Sound and Fury," Education column, *The New York Times*, May 19, 1963.

[*69*]

PENFIELD, WILDER, "The Uncommitted Cortex, The Child's Changing Brain," *Atlantic* Magazine, July, 1964.

[*70*]

KRAMER, RITA, "Family Business in Brief," *The New York Times Magazine*, Jan. 3, 1965.

[*71*]

BLOOM, BENJAMIN S., *Stability and Change in Human Characteristics*, New York, 1964.

[*72*]

"Human Communication," Brochure issued by National Institute of Child Health and Human Development. Bethesda, Maryland, 1965.

Chapter VI

[73]
WALLACE, KARL R. et al., *History of Speech Education in America,*
New York, 1954. Material for this chapter draws heavily on this work.

[73]
REID, RONALD F. "The Boylston Professorship of Rhetoric and Ora-
tory, 1806–1904: A Case Study in Changing Concepts of Rhetoric and
Pedagogy," *Quarterly Journal of Speech,* Oct., 1959.

[74]
ANDERSON, DOROTHY I., "Edward T. Channing's Definition of
Rhetoric," *Speech Monographs,* 1947, pp. 81–92.

[75]
BROOKS, VAN WYCK, *The Flowering of New England,* New York,
1936.

[76]
TYSON, RAYMOND W. "The Public Speaking of James Russell Lowell
in England," *The Southern Speech Journal,* Vol. XXVIII, No. 1, Fall,
1962.

[76]
MORISON, SAMUEL ELIOT. *The Development of Harvard University,*
Cambridge, 1930.

[77]
Letter from William H. Pinkerton, News Office, Harvard University,
Dec. 4, 1964.

[80]
COMMAGER, HENRY STEELE, *The American Mind,* New Haven, 1950,
p. 24.

[80]
Book Review: "Bode, Carl, *The American Lyceum: Town Meeting
of the Mind,* Oxford U. Press, 1956," in *Quarterly Journal of Speech,*
Oct., 1956.

[81]
BROOKS, VAN WYCK, *The Life of Emerson,* New York, 1932.

[82]
GRAY, GILES WILKERSON, "What Was Elocution?" *Quarterly Journal of Speech,* Feb. 1960.

[88]
"Column One," Editorial in *Today's Speech,* Sept., 1963.

[88]
BOSMAJIAN, HAIG A., Letter to "The Forum." *The Speech Teacher,*
Vol. XI, No. 3, Sept., 1962, p. 253.

[88]

WILEY, EARL, "Special Knowledge and the Rhetorical Continuum," *Quarterly Journal of Speech*, Dec., 1959.

[90]

ARNOLD, CARROLL C., "The Case Against Speech: An Examination of Critical Viewpoints," *Quarterly Journal of Speech*, April, 1954.

[90]

REID, LOREN, "The President's Page," *Quarterly Journal of Speech*, April, 1957.

[90]

ROSS, HAROLD R., "Teach Them Anything But Not Speech," *Today's Speech*, Feb., 1961.

[90]

PETRIE, CHARLES R., "In Defense of Speech," *Today's Speech*, Nov., 1961.

[90]

DAHLE, THOMAS L., "Speech—What Is It?" *Today's Speech*, Sept., 1963.

[91]

"The Field of Speech: Its Purpose and Scope in Education," Special statement, Speech Association of America, 1963.

[92]

"Manifesto on the Status of the Speech Association of America," Executive Committee of the Speech Association of America Administrative Council, 1965.

Chapter VII

[93]

LONGGOOD, WILLIAM, *Talking Your Way To Success—The Story of the Dale Carnegie Course*, New York, 1962.

[94]

The Dale Carnegie Course in Effective Speaking and Human Relations, 23rd Edition, Dale Carnegie & Associates, Inc., New York, 1960, 1962.

[96]

DAVIE, FRANCES E. X., "An Analysis of the Speech Programs in 108 Selected Evening Colleges in the United States," *Speech Monographs*, June, 1960, p. 149.

[97]

EMERSON, RALPH WALDO, "Eloquence."

[*97*]
BRIGANCE, WILLIAM NORWOOD, *Speech, Its Techniques and Disciplines in a Free Society*, New York, 1952.

[*97*]
HARRINGTON, ELBERT W., "The Role of Speech in Liberal Education," *Quarterly Journal of Speech*, Oct., 1955.

[*99*]
BRADEN, WALDO W., "Putting Rigor Into The Teaching of Speech," *Today's Speech*, Sept., 1963.

[*100*]
DIETRICH, JOHN ERT and BROOKS, KEITH, *Practical Speaking for the Technical Man*, Englewood Cliffs, 1958.

[*101*]
Book Review: "Van Dusen, C. Raymond and Smith, Howard Van, *The New Speech-O-Gram Technique For Persuasive Public Speaking*, Englewood Cliffs, 1962," in *Quarterly Journal of Speech*, Oct., 1963, p. 347.

[*102*]
ELAM, PAUL. "An Investigation to Determine the Extent to Which Speech Influences the Selection of Employees." M.A. Thesis, College of the Pacific, 1952, published in *Speech Monographs*, Aug., 1953.

[*102*]
ZELKO, HAROLD P. "Practical Training In Effective Speaking." *Training Directors*, Jan., 1958.

[*104*]
ZELKO, HAROLD P. "Books and Materials for Business and Professional Speech Training," *Today's Speech*, Nov., 1963.

[*106*]
RANDALL, CLARENCE B., "Speak Up!" *Think* Magazine, May, 1962.

[*106*]
SYLVESTER, W. A. "Beware of the Expert Speech Maker," *Chemical Engineering*, Aug. 8, 1960.

[*106*]
Pamphlet describing "Executive Action" Course offered by American Management Association, 1959–60.

Chapter VIII

[*108*]
HITLER, ADOLF. *Mein Kampf*, Translated by Helmut Ripperger, New York, 1939.

[*109*]

BOSMAJIAN, HAIG A. "The Nazi Speaker's Rhetoric," *Quarterly Journal of Speech*, Dec., 1960.

[*109*]

SCANLON, ROSS, "The Nazi Party Speaker System," *Speech Monographs*, Aug., 1949.

[*109*]

VON MOLTKE, HENRY. "Joseph Goebbels: Chief Spokesman for the Third Reich," Abstract of Ph.D. dissertation, *Speech Monographs*, June, 1962.

[*109*]

CASMIR, FRED L., "The Power of Oral Communication," *Today's Speech*, Nov., 1962.

[*115*]

IEZZI, FRANK, "Benito Mussolini, Crowd Psychologist," *Quarterly Journal of Speech*, Vol. 45, 1959, p. 166.

[*115*]

CASMIR, FRED L., "The Hitler I Heard," *Quarterly Journal of Speech*, Feb., 1963, p. 8.

[*118*]

WEAVER, ANDREW THOMAS, "Toward Understanding Through Speech," *Vital Speeches*, Feb. 1, 1961.

[*119*]

T.R.B. from Washington, "Looking Back," *The New Republic*, Nov. 7, 1964.

Chapter IX

[*121*]

STITES, WILLIAM HARRISON, "The Place of Effective, Responsible and Intelligent Speaking in the Rhetorics and the Societies of Classical and Early Modern Cultures," *Speech Monographs*, Aug., 1955, p. 167.

[*121*]

RASMUS, WARD. "Voice and Diction: Historical Perspective," *Quarterly Journal of Speech*, Oct. 1961.

[*122*]

MAYER, MARTIN, *Madison Avenue, U.S.A.*, New York, 1958.

[*124*]

SMITH, TERRY, "Bobby's Image," *Esquire* Magazine, April 1965.

[*126*]

HAIMAN, FRANKLYN S., "Democratic Ethics and the Hidden Persuaders," *Quarterly Journal of Speech*, Dec., 1958.

[*126*]
NILSEN, THOMAS R. "Free Speech, Persuasion and the Democratic Process," *Quarterly Journal of Speech*, Oct., 1958.

[*128*]
BECKER, SAMUEL L., "Presidential Power: Influence of Broadcasting," *Quarterly Journal of Speech*, Feb., 1961.

[*129*]
Executive Order No. 10501, Nov. 5, 1953, "Safeguarding Official Information In The Interests of the Defense of the United States."

[*129*]
STEVENS, LEONARD A., "Top-Secret Mania." *The Nation*, Oct. 12, 1963.

[*130*]
MORGENTHAU, HANS J. "War With China?" *The New Republic*, April 3, 1965.

[*131*]
ZIEGELMUELLER, GEORGE W., "A Study of the Speaking of Conservatives in Opposition to the New Deal," *Speech Monographs*, Aug., 1963.

[*131*]
DEBOER, MARVIN EUGENE, "A Rhetorical Analysis of Selected Addresses of the National Commanders of The American Legion, 1919–1954," *Speech Monographs*, Aug., 1963.

[*131*]
MCKEE, SISTER MARY JULIANUS. "Congresswoman Clare Boothe Luce: Her Rhetoric Against Communism." *Speech Monographs*, Aug., 1963.

[*131*]
Letter from Walter W. Stevens, University of Washington, *Quarterly Journal of Speech*, Oct., 1961.

[*132*]
" 'Abolition' Postscript." Editorial in *The Minneapolis Star*, Feb. 27, 1961.

[*132*]
"Operation Abolition," Editorial, *The New York Times*, May 8, 1961.

[*132*]
ANDERSON, C. G., "Rhetoric On The Right," Special Paper prepared at Danbury State College, Danbury, Conn., 1962, Unpublished.

[*134*]
"Six Reasons Why You Should Worry About Extremism in the U.S. Today," Advertisement by National Council for Civic Responsibility of The Public Affairs Institute, *The New York Times*, Oct. 8, 1964.

[*134*]
CHURCH, FRANK, U.S. Senator from Idaho. "Conspiracy USA," *Look,*
Jan. 26, 1965.

[*134*]
Speeches by Senator Thomas H. Kuchel, *Congressional Record,*
May 2, 1963, May 28, 1963.

[*135*]
STERN, LAWRENCE, "A Town Where Everything's Right," The *Washington Post,* Nov. 29, 1964.

[*135*]
STERN, LAWRENCE, "Hanging President In Effigy Is Oil Town's Idea
of Fun," Chicago *Sun-Times,* Nov. 29, 1964.

[*136*]
RESTON, JAMES, "Oxford, Miss.: The Conflict of Memory and Ambition," *The New York Times,* March 5, 1965.

[*138*]
"Testing Whether That Nation," 41st Annual Report of the American Civil Liberties Union, New York, July 1, 1960–June 30, 1961.

Chapter X

[*140*]
NUCCIO, SAUL, "Advertising: The Spurious Foot in the Door." *The New York Times,* Oct. 21, 1964.

[*141*]
Letter from Robert D. Calkins, President, The Brookings Institution, Washington, D.C. to Robert G. Gunderson, Executive Vice-President, Speech Association of America, Dec. 7, 1961. Quoted by permission from Mr. Calkins.

[*141*]
DOUGLAS, U.S. SUPREME COURT JUSTICE WILLIAM O. First Annual
Lecture for the Earl Warren Institute on Ethics and Human Relations,
University of Judaism, Los Angeles, Calif., quoted in *Des Moines Register,* July 2, 1962.

[*143*]
LYND, ROBERT S. *Middletown.* As quoted by Cook, Fred J. "The
Corrupt Society." *The Nation,* June 18, 1963.

[*145*]
ARNOLD, CHRISTIAN K., "Tips on Using Ghostwriters," *The Management Review,* May, 1963.

[*145*]
BART, PETER. "The Busy Ghosts," *Saturday Review,* Sept. 14, 1963.

[*145*]
BORMANN, ERNEST G., "Ethics of Ghostwritten Speeches," *Quarterly Journal of Speech*, Oct., 1961.

[*146*]
OBERDORFER, DON. "Vast Ghostland of Washington." *The New York Times Magazine*, April 26, 1964.

[*148*]
BORMANN, ERNEST G., "Ghostwriting and The Rhetorical Critic," *Quarterly Journal of Speech*, Oct., 1960.

[*150*]
WINDES, RUSSELL, JR. "Stevenson's Speech Staff in the 1956 Campaign." *Quarterly Journal of Speech*, Feb., 1960.

[*152*]
GRALA, WILLIAM L., "Industry's Best Defense: The Speaker's Bureau," *Public Relations Journal*, Sept., 1964.

[*154*]
"Speakers Bureau Tells Chrysler's Story," *Printer's Ink*, Dec 12, 1958.

[*156*]
RIPLEY, JOSEPH M., JR., "The Practices and Policies Regarding Broadcasts of Opinions about Controversial Issues by Radio and Television Stations in the United States," *Speech Monographs*, June, 1962, Vol. 29.

Chapter XI

[*160*]
KATZ, ELIHU and LAZARASFELD, PAUL F. *Personal Influence*, Glencoe, Ill., 1955.

[*161*]
SCHRAMM, WILBUR, *Responsibility in Mass Communication*, New York, 1957.

[*161*]
PORTER, WILLIAM E. "Does Man Still Control His Own Mind?" *The Iowa Quest* (State University of Iowa School of Journalism) June, 1961.

[*163*]
LAZARASFELD, PAUL, et al., *People's Choice*, Columbia University Press, New York, 1948.

[*169*]
NEWCOMB, ROBERT and SAMMONS, MARG. *Speak Up, Management*, New York, 1951.

[*169*]
PETERS, RAYMOND, *Communication Within Industry,* New York, 1950.

[*169*]
FISHER, FRANK E., "A New Look at Management Communication," *Personnel,* May 1955.

[*169*]
PIERSALL, DARRELL T., "A Case Study of Oral Communication Practices of Foremen in a Mid-Western Corporation," *Speech Monographs,* June, 1956.

[*170*]
LEWIS, GUSTAF IRWIN, "A Survey of Management Attitudes Regarding Oral Communication Needs and Practices in Large Industries of Los Angeles County," *Speech Monographs,* Aug., 1955.

[*171*]
HENRY, DAVID D., "Concern for Consensus," *Quarterly Journal of Speech,* Oct., 1961.

Chapter XII

[*174*]
DEWEY, JOHN, *Democracy and Education,* New York, 1916.

[*174*]
CLAPP, JOHN M., "The Place of English in American Life," Report of the National Council of Teachers of English, Chicago, 1926.

[*175*]
HATFIELD, W. WILBUR, "An Experience Curriculum in English," *English Monographs,* No. 4, National Council of the Teachers of English, New York, 1935.

[*175*]
RANKIN, PAUL T., "Listening Ability," Proceedings of the Ohio State Educational Conference, Ohio State University, Columbus, 1939, pp. 172–183.

[*175*]
SMITH, DORA V., "Instruction in English," Monograph No. 20, Bulletin 17, U.S. Office of Education, 1932.

[*175*]
SMITH, DORA V. "Summary of New York Regents Inquiry," *The English Journal,* March, 1939.

[*176*]
"The Field of Speech; Its Purposes and Scope in Education," Speech Association of America, New York, 1963.

[*177*]
CONANT, JAMES BRYANT, *The Education of American Teachers,*
New York, 1963.

[*177*]
BYER, BURTON H., "Speech in Teacher Education," Unpublished
dissertation for Doctor of Education Degree, Teachers College, Columbia University, 1957.

[*180*]
EHRLICH, PHYLLIS, "Children Said to Imitate Parents' Speech Habits," *The New York Times,* June 13, 1962.

[*180*]
SCHREIBER, FLORA RHETA, "How to Talk With Children," *Today's
Speech,* April 1963.

[*181*]
BARBARA, DOMINICK A. "Listening With a Modest Ear," *Today's
Speech,* Feb. 1961.

[*181*]
BARBARA, DOMINICK A. "The Struggle for Emotional Survival," *Today's Speech,* April, 1963.

[*182*]
HUCKLEBERRY, ALAN W., "The Relationship Between Change in
Speech Proficiency and Change in Student Teacher Proficiency," ab-
stracted thesis, *Speech Monographs,* Nov. 1950.

[*183*]
Letter from Alan Reitman, Associate Director, American Civil Liberties Union, New York, Aug. 12, 1963.

[*183*]
SHIFF, ROBERT A., "Presidents and Paperwork," *Duns Review and
Modern Industry,* April 1959.

[*183*]
SHIFF, ROBERT A. and NEGUS, ALAN, "Let's Stress Information, Not
Pieces of Paper," Office Management Yearbook, Jan. 1959.

[*185*]
MICHALAK, JOSEPH, "The Place of Controversy on the College Campus," New York *Herald Tribune,* April 25, 1965.

[*188*]
MASON, OLGA, "Procedure in Retrospect," *Parliamentary Journal,*
June 1964.

[*191*]
WALSH, MICHAEL P., S.J., "Values In Education—Brilliance Alone
Has Proven To Be Not Enough," *Vital Speeches,* June 1960.

[*191*]
CURRIVAN, GENE, "Catholic Educator Decries Conformity," *The New York Times,* April 23, 1965.

[*192*]
BAKER, VIRGIL L. and EUBANKS, RALPH T., "Democracy: Challenge to Rhetorical Education," *Quarterly Journal of Speech,* Feb. 1960.

[*193*]
EUBANKS, RALPH T., "Toward an Axiology of Rhetoric," *Quarterly Journal of Speech,* April 1962.

[*194*]
BREWSTER, LAWRENCE W., "An Exploratory Study of Some Aspects of Critical Listening Among College Freshmen," Unpublished Doctor's Dissertation, State University of Iowa, June 1956.

[*195*]
TAME, ELLWOOD R., "An Analytical Study of the Relationship Between Ability in Critical Thinking and Ability in Contest Debate and Discussion," *Speech Monographs,* June 1959.

[*195*]
BREMBECK, WINSTON L., "The Effects of a Course in Argumentation on Critical Thinking Ability," *Speech Monographs,* Sept. 1949.

[*195*]
HARRINGTON, ELBERT W., "The Role of Speech in Liberal Education," *Quarterly Journal of Speech,* Oct. 1955.

[*197*]
NICHOLS, RALPH G. "Factors Accounting for Differences in Comprehension of Materials Presented Orally in the Classroom," unpublished doctor's dissertation, State University of Iowa, 1948.

[*197*]
NICHOLS, RALPH G. and STEVENS, LEONARD A., *Are You Listening,* New York, 1957.

General References Chapter XII

HURST, CHARLES G., JR., "Speech and Functional Intelligence: An Experimental Study of Educational Implications of a Basic Speech Course," *Speech Monographs,* June 1962.

MARKGRAF, BRUCE, "Listening Pedagogy In Teacher-Training Institutions," *The Journal of Communication,* March 1962.

OLBRICHT, THOMAS H., "Speech and Commitment," *Today's Speech,* April 1964.

SMITH, ROBERT W., "The Rhetoric of Commitment," Letter, *Quarterly Journal of Speech,* April 1963.

WIEMAN, HENRY NELSON and WALTER, OTIS M. "Toward an Analysis of Ethics for Rhetoric," *Quarterly Journal of Speech,* Oct. 1957.

WILT, MARIAM E. Listeninig in Classrooms, *Elementary English,* May 1949.

Index

ABOUT THE AUTHOR

Mr. Stevens is the co-author of *Are You Listening?* and a forthcoming book about travel and money. He is the author of *Jet Flight 808* and *Old Peppersass*. He has been a freelance magazine writer for fourteen years, and his articles have appeared in *The Saturday Evening Post, The Nation, Pageant, Coronet, True,* and *The Reader's Digest*. He is married, with four children, and resides in Bridgeport, Connecticut.

Ralph G. Nichols, who wrote the Introduction, is head of the Department of Rhetoric at the University of Minnesota (St. Paul Campus). A former president of the Speech Association of America, he holds a Ph.D. in speech from the University of Iowa. He is co-author of *Are You Listening?*